Linda:

I saw this at the store and I th... ♡ what it would make the perfect "Just Because" gift! When I saw that GN'R ♪ were in the metal Classics section, I KNEW I had to get it!

Enjoy!

Love John
xoxox

THE BEST OF
METAL

‖‖‖‖‖‖‖‖‖‖‖‖‖‖‖
W9-BME-447

THE BEST OF

METAL
The Essential CD Guide

**PAUL ELLIOTT
& JON HOTTEN**

CollinsPublishersSanFrancisco
A Division of HarperCollins*Publishers*

First published in the United States in 1993 by Collins Publishers San Francisco,
1160 Battery Street, San Francisco, California 94111

Library of Congress Cataloging-in-Publication Data

Elliott, Paul.
    The best of metal : the essential CD guide / Paul Elliott & Jon Hotten.
       p.   cm. — (The Essential CD guides)
    Discography: p.
    Includes index.
    ISBN 0-00-255336-8
    1. Rock musicians—Biography—Dictionaries. 2. Heavy metal
(Music)—History and criticism. 3. Compact discs—Reviews.
I. Hotten, Jon. II. Title. III. Series.
ML 102.R6E44   1993
781.66—dc20

                                      93-11543
                                        CIP
                                        MN

Printed in Great Britain

THE AUTHORS

Paul Elliott is News Editor for the UK's leading heavy metal magazine, *Kerrang!*
Previously he has worked for *Sounds*, *Vox*, and *Zigzag*, and has contributed to
several rock yearbooks. His first book, an unofficial biography of Guns N' Roses,
was published by Morrow in 1990.
Jon Hotten is Editor of *RAW*, the UK's biggest-selling hard rock bi-weekly.
Previously he worked as Acquisitions Editor for *Kerrang!*

Contents

INTRODUCTION

†††

HEAVY METAL IS AN AGEING TERM WHICH CANNOT TRULY EMBRACE MUSIC AS DISPARATE AS SLAYER'S BRUTAL THRASH AND JOURNEY'S LUSH SOFT-ROCK. FOR THE FAN, HEAVY METAL GOES BEYOND MUSIC AND INTO A LIFESTYLE. FOR ITS STRONGEST OPPONENTS, IT'S A DENSE AND UNINTELLIGIBLE RACKET, A DARK CULT IMBUED WITH IMAGES OF DOOM.

Heavy metal is vast. It can be awesome, in Led Zeppelin's majestic blues power or Black Sabbath's elemental grind. It can be hilarious, in Thor's ludicrous feats of strength, or Krokus's dumb, sex-rock machismo, and it can be both, in Judas Priest's machine-gun riffs and tongue-in-cheek, metaphysical tales of rampaging Hellions and avenging metal gods. Heavy metal can laugh at itself too. *This Is Spinal Tap* is a wicked satire, a giant belly-laugh of a film with its humour rooted in an in-depth knowledge of, and an abiding affection for, the music, its absurdities and its pathos.

Heavy metal has its gods; from the flaxen-haired British wailer Robert Plant, through the exuberant showman "Diamond" David Lee Roth and the moody, pouting Nikki Sixx, to the all-American pin-up boy Jon Bon Jovi and that charming rogue, the late Bon Scott. It has its devils and devilry, too; from Glen Benton, Deicide's unrepentant Satanist, to Slayer's ghoulish document on Nazi butcher Josef Mengele, 'Angel Of Death'. Heavy metal has characters; from the shaven-headed, leather-bound Rob Halford to the grand old madman of metal Ozzy Osbourne, from eternal schoolboy Angus Young to the lavishly costumed Kiss and the grouchy and acid-tongued Saxon frontman Biff Byford.

In the Nineties, heavy metal has two of the biggest-grossing, headline-making, stadium-filling, multimedia superstars, San Franciscan riffmeisters Metallica and Los Angeles bad boys Guns N' Roses, who are fronted by the modern-day Mick Jagger, W. Axl Rose.

Heavy metal has real women stars, too. No longer chained by the genre's seemingly inherent sexism, L7 and Babes In Toyland offer an alternative to the stereotypical rock chick like Lita Ford.

Finally, heavy metal has a cutting edge. The Seattle-rooted grunge scene boasts the hottest cross-over acts—Nirvana, Pearl Jam, Soundgarden—and the new giants, Alice In Chains. Jane's Addiction were pointed, committed and graceful rebels, Ice-T's Body Count had a president speak against them.

Heavy metal is no longer about demons, dragons and bad haircuts, if it ever was. For all the limp copyists making a living, there are as many great musicians making big, fast, loud, mad, funny and passionate music.

One book could not cover all that ground, and this book does not pretend to try. An exhaustive history of heavy metal would be thick enough to make a decent footstool, and would probably be about as interesting. Much heavy metal is totally forgettable, a vague imitation of the real thing. Guns N' Roses's blistering début, *Appetite For Destruction*, has been badly impersonated by myriad wannabes. Slayer's extremes have legion copyists, AC/DC's simple yet devastating bar-room boogie has been exhaustively reproduced by thousands. Bands defined and limited by their heroes have been excluded.

Included are the 110 most significant heavy metal artists of the past 25 years, from left-field cult acts to mega grossing rock legends. The greatest and most influential albums are reassessed, and not just the million-sellers like AC/DC's *Back In Black*, Def Leppard's *Hysteria* and Nirvana's *Nevermind*. Jane's Addiction were dissolved by enigmatic leader Perry Farrell while on the brink of major success, but created on their third album *Ritual De Lo Habitual* some of the most powerful and strangely beautiful hard rock music ever recorded. Texan trio King's X have sold just a handful of each of their four albums, yet their *Out Of The Silent Plant* remains one of the greatest rock débuts of all time.

Former Deep Purple and Whitesnake singer David Coverdale and ex Led Zeppelin guitarist Jimmy Page came together in 1993 and launched their unlikely supergroup project with a spectacular epic heavy rock album, simply titled *Coverdale/Page*.

The root of heavy metal's appeal is the power of a loud electric guitar. Every year, a number of hard rock songs crush all barriers of style and taste to become hit singles, definitive sounds of the age; songs like Black Sabbath's 'Paranoid', Guns N' Roses's 'Sweet Child O' Mine', Bon Jovi's 'Livin' On A Prayer', ZZ Top's 'Gimme All Your Lovin' ', Whitesnake's 'Here I Go Again', Nirvana's 'Smells Like Teen Spirit', Survivor's 'Eye Of The Tiger'—the list is endless.

Metal has also been used to pump up the volume in dance music. Following the lead of rappers Run DMC, who covered Aerosmith's 'Walk This Way', the lecherous Tone Loc made a career out of recycling riffs by Montrose, Van Halen and Kiss.

Heavy metal has never really been in vogue; even Nirvana's Kurt Cobain, cover star of every major metal magazine, loathes generic traditional metal. Heavy metal is beyond fashion, which is perhaps its greatest strength. As Judas Priest declared in the definitive statement on the genre, simply and classically titled 'Heavy Metal': "It will survive against all odds, stampeding on forever!" Or something like that.

THRASH

The Ultra-violence

THE THRASH BOOM OF THE MID-EIGHTIES WAS A GOLDEN AGE FOR HEAVY METAL. THE NEW WAVE OF BRITISH HEAVY METAL (NWOBHM) HAD ENCOURAGED YOUNG BANDS TO MAKE HEADWAY VIA INDEPENDENT RECORD LABELS, BUT BY 1983, THE BIGGER NWOBHM ACTS WERE PART OF THE ESTABLISHMENT AND THE LESSER LIGHTS HAD MOSTLY FADED ALTOGETHER: IRON MAIDEN HAD SCORED A NUMBER 1 ALBUM IN THE UK, DEF LEPPARD WERE SUPERSTARS IN THE US, WHILE THE LIKES OF SAMSON, PRAYING MANTIS AND ANGELWITCH WERE EITHER DEAD OR BREATHING THEIR LAST.

However, one NWOBHM band were seen as pioneers of thrash, a new metal subgenre. Venom, three young men from the north-east of England, played heavy metal of an unprecedented savagery. Mixing the speed of Motorhead with the lo-fi grunge and tacky occultist imagery of Black Sabbath, Venom created black metal. This metal was indeed blacker and more horrible than any before it. *Welcome To Hell*, the trio's début album, was described upon its release in 1981 as "possibly the heaviest record ever allowed into the shops". It is also arguably *the* seminal thrash album, with heavy punk outfit Discharge's *Hear Nothing, See Nothing, Say Nothing* a close second. Thrash was simply heavy metal with the speed-thrill of punk and hardcore.

Metallica, the most important and successful band to emerge from the thrash explosion, cite Venom as a major influence. In the early Eighties Metallica frequently supported Venom, but by the middle of the decade Venom had lost the plot and were usurped by thrash's so-called "big four": Metallica, Anthrax, Slayer and Megadeth.

Metallica's 1983 début *Kill 'Em All* was the harbinger of thrash, and is a classic example of the genre. This and the band's second album *Ride The Lightning* did much to define the famous Bay Area sound. Metallica's hometown, San Francisco, was to thrash what Seattle is to grunge, spawning a sound all its own—a monstrous "crunch"—and a large number of great bands including Exodus, Megadeth, Testament, Possessed and the precocious Death Angel, whose drummer Gus Pepa was just 14 when they cut their début album *The Ultra Violence*. Exodus's *Bonded By Blood* is another classic Bay Area thrash release, a work of unremitting brutality executed with astonishing precision,

although after the departure of Paul Baloff, a cult Bay Area figure with a genuinely terrifying scream, Exodus lost their bite.

Megadeth were formed by scowling, flame-haired guitarist/vocalist Dave Mustaine after he left Metallica. The group's music was as dark as Mustaine's demeanour. The first album, grimly-titled *Killing Is My Business...And Business is Good*, included a new arrangement of Metallica's 'The Four Horsemen', retitled 'Mechanix', plus a reworking of Nancy Sinatra's 'These Boots Are Made For Walking'. And when Mustaine spat the line: "one of these days these boots are gonna walk all over you", it didn't sound like he was kidding!

Megadeth's second album, this time cynically titled *Peace Sells...But Who's Buying?*, is one of the nastiest heavy metal records ever released. Subsequent albums have brought the band a degree of mainstream success as Mustaine has kicked hard

drugs, but *Peace Sells* remains his most intense work.

Comparatively, Anthrax appear cartoonish. Latterly the New Yorkers have packed away their bermuda shorts and have quit much of their buffoonery, but the image of Anthrax as the clowns of thrash persists. Perhaps it was unwise of them to celebrate their love of rap music by goofing off with 'I'm The Man', a wearisome parody.

James Hetfield, guitarist/vocalist for San Franciscan thrash pioneers Metallica.

Jeff Hanneman (left) and Kerry King: Slayer's evil twin guitarists.

Nevertheless, Anthrax have made some fine records, with 1987's *Among The Living* producing the grinding single 'I Am The Law'.

Of the big four, Metallica have achieved the greatest success, but the ultimate thrash metal band are Los Angeleans Slayer, who created in *Reign In Blood* the metal album to end all metal albums. Slayer's début *Show No Mercy*, released in 1983, was amateurish, adolescent Satanic speed metal, but its successor, *Hell Awaits,* was both powerful and frightening. On 'Praise Of Death', bassist/vocalist Tom Araya roars in one huge gulp of air: "Running and hunting and slashing and crushing and searching and seeing and stabbing and shooting and thrashing and smashing and burning destroying and killing and bleeding and pleading then death!"

Reign In Blood followed, and drove metal to its ultimate extreme. If 'Praise Of Death', 'Necrophiliac' and 'Kill Again' were shocking, 'Angel Of Death', which recounts the wartime atrocities of Nazi butcher Josef Mengele, was simply nauseating. 'Angel Of Death' is also the definitive thrash track, combining insanely fast riffs with still heavier slow passages. Two more albums, *South Of Heaven* and *Seasons In The Abyss*, have stalled Slayer's title as the heaviest band on the planet.

If Europe had a Bay Area, it was the Ruhr district of Germany, a network of steel towns where thrash audiences are reckoned to be the most over-zealous in the world. Kreator, Destruction and Sodom typified the dizzying, clanking German speed metal sound, Kreator's *Pleasure To Kill* the classic study. Kreator were signed by the Noise label, which specialized in extreme new metal. Also on the label's roster were French Canadians Voivod, who described their own sound as akin to that of heavy machinery! Voivod's conceptual,

sci-fi-fixated and psychedelic "industrial metal" peaked on 1988's *Dimension Hatross*, although for sheer power, the title of the second album, *RRRROOOOAAAARRRR*, speaks volumes.

Celtic Frost were also on Noise and were the most bizarre of the thrash generation. Based in Switzerland, the band formed from the remnants of Hellhammer, who were dubbed the worst band in the world after the release of their sole recording *Apocalyptic Raids*.

Frost were the original death metal band, but they alienated much of their hardcore fan base with two ambitious records, 1987's *Into The Pandemonium*—an extraordinary, brilliant work mixing heavy riffing with hip-hop, spoken French poetry and a death march—and 1988's *Cold Lake*, on which Celtic Frost front-man Tom G. Warrior wore lipgloss and played monstrously heavy cock rock!

As with the NWOBHM, the big four are now mainstream acts, while thrash itself has been made obsolete by death and industrial metal.

GLAM

"Look What the Cat Dragged In"

KISS MAY HAVE WORN THE MOST MAKE-UP, BUT THEY ARE NOT THE ONLY METAL ACT TO GRAB HEADLINES BY DRESSING UP LIKE THEIR BIG SISTERS. OVER THE PAST TWO DECADES BANDS AS DIVERSE AS THE NEW YORK DOLLS AND POISON HAVE DEVELOPED PROVOCATIVE ANDROGYNOUS IMAGES WITH VARYING DEGREES OF SUCCESS.

Glam rock's roots are in the Seventies when, in the UK, the charts were dominated by men in lipstick and glitzy girl's clothes. The movement's leaders were Gary Glitter, Mud, T. Rex, the Sweet and Slade.

And while Britain rocked to glam party anthems, the New York Dolls and Alice Cooper were shocking the US. The Dolls looked simply outrageous in thrift store hooker chic, stackheeled boots and crudely-styled make-up. Junkies? Transvestites? Whatever, the New York Dolls just looked bad. The look has been much imitated.

While Alice Cooper is a seminal glam rock figure, his own image was so freakish and over-the-top, it went far beyond mere "glam". Cooper and Kiss were the princes of rock theatre. Where most glam rockers were simple party animals, Cooper was a satirist, but however loaded with irony, songs like 'Welcome To My Nightmare' and 'Elected' were hugely popular rock songs,

Kiss circa 1981: the ultimate rock image.

and the gloriously anarchic 'School's Out' spawned a hundred weak imitations; schoolyard rebellion is a staple of glam rock.

In the Eighties, glam came back into vogue, notably in Los Angeles, where the local heavy metal scene appeared to be populated exclusively by cock rockers in spandex and lipstick. Big hair was everywhere. Motley Crue emerged as the kings of Hollywood glam metal at the turn of the Eighties. The quartet put out their début LP *Too Fast For Love* via their own Leathur label in 1981 and instantly became the darlings of a scene which also produced Ratt, Black N' Blue, Quiet Riot and Dokken. The album is a classic glam recording, its raw low-

budget production perfect for the heavy bubblegum metal of 'Live Wire', 'Red Hot', etc. Bassist and chief songwriter Nikki Sixx was tutored in rock 'n' roll exploitation by Kim Fowley, who had previously created dubious all-girl pop rock act the Runaways. Hence Motley Crue's second album *Shout At The Devil* boasted a pentagram on the cover and a song entitled 'God Save The Children Of The Beast'. The Crue's music was still basic riffy party rock, but the whisper of satanism gave the band an element of danger and mystique which, allied to their reputation for excessive indulgence in sex, drink and drugs, made Motley Crue the most talked about new metal act in America.

Disaster struck the band just before Christmas of 1984. Singer Vince Neil crashed a car in Los Angeles, killing his passenger Razzle, English-born drummer of Finnish glam rock 'n' rollers Hanoi Rocks. Neil escaped with a mere 30 days' imprisonment and compensation fees of $2.6 million, and the Crue carried on to make three more albums, two of them US Number 1s, before Neil was ousted. His replacement, John Corabi, formerly of the Scream, has a lot to live up to. If a poor singer, Neil was a charismatic frontman. He has since embarked on a solo career.

Vince Neil got over the death of Razzle, but Hanoi Rocks did not. The band had just made their first album for CBS and had seemed destined for superstardom, when Razzle died. Hanoi Rocks cut four independently-released albums, including the classic trash rock of *Self Destruction Blues* and *Back To Mystery City*, and one for CBS, *Two Steps From The Move*, before Razzle's death broke their spirit. The albums have been reissued in the US via Guns N' Roses's own Uzi Suicide label. Axl Rose is a huge fan of the band.

Guns N' Roses were also dubbed "glam" back in 1987. On the sleeve of the band's début EP 'Live Like A Suicide', Rose's hair is teased up, but the band soon reverted to a tougher image. Lately, Poison have also toned down their glam look, but in the mid-Eighties they succeeded the Motley Crue as the new kings of LA glam.

Poison's début *Look What The Cat Dragged In* is a supreme glam metal album. The music is pure pop rock in the style of Cheap Trick, if witless by comparison. 'Talk Dirty To Me' and the title cut are typical Poison anthems, as frothy as a tall shake, as one reviewer remarked. Successive albums have seen the band mature; on 1990's *Flesh And Blood*, singer Bret Michaels wrote a piano-led ballad, 'Something To Believe In', inspired by the death of his bodyguard through drug abuse. By 1992, loud-mouthed but technically limited guitarist C. C. DeVille was replaced by neo-classical axe progidy Richie Kotzen, and the band posed for photographs in jeans, minus lipstick and eyeliner.

The Eighties also briefly starred Twisted Sister and Wrathchild. The former were burly New Yorkers in drag, the latter self-titled "stack-heeled strutters" from the English town of Evesham. Both were hilarious. After all, glam was meant to be fun.

FUNK METAL

Headbangin' and Bootyshakin'

WHEN PRINCE BECAME THE BIGGEST CROSSOVER ACT OF 1984 WITH THE WATERSHED *PURPLE RAIN* ALBUM, THE SONG THAT WON OVER HARD ROCK FANS WAS 'LET'S GO CRAZY', A CLASSIC EXAMPLE OF FUNK METAL. PRINCE IS A GREAT GUITARIST WHO LOVES TO SHOW OFF WITH HEAVY METAL PYROTECHNICS, AND 'LET'S GO CRAZY' IS FULL OF THE STUFF; THE REVOLUTION EVEN CUT THE POWER-FUNK RIFF FOR THEIR LEADER TO LAUNCH INTO A WILD SOLO.

Prince, whose 'Let's Go Crazy' is one of the great funk metal tracks.

Prince has mixed funk and metal before and after 1984—on 1979's 'Bambi' and 1989's 'Electric Chair'—but 'Let's Go Crazy' is his perfect marriage of dance rhythm and rock power.

The funk metal hybrid has produced some of the most powerful and colourful music of the past 20 years, by both black and white artists, and frequently by multi-racial bands. Jimi Hendrix, arguably the greatest rock guitarist of all time yet strangely the sole black rock guitar legend, created fluid, freeform hard rock music, but little of it was really funky. Hendrix's former employers the Isley Brothers played a more tangible heavy funk rock fusion, tracks like 'That Lady' boasting flashy rock guitar licks teased out over hot Seventies funk riffs. Similarly, the Ohio Players toughened up their funk with some serious guitar action, notably on 'Fopp', which was later covered by Seattle metal act Soundgarden. Soundgarden singer Chris Cornell described the Ohio Players as "the Kiss of funk"! Van Halen also used to cover a Players' tune, 'Fire'. Crazy funk godfather George Clinton fulfilled his rock fantasies through Funkadelic. While best known for their worldwide disco hit 'One Nation Under A Groove', Funkadelic have cut some killer rock tracks, such as 'Super Stupid' and 'Maggot Brain', the latter a 10-minute orgy of blissed-out FX-laden hard rock guitar pyrotechnics.

Mother's Finest are reckoned by many to be the greatest funk rock band of them all. From Atlanta, Georgia, they are fronted by phenomenal singer Joyce "Baby Jean" Kennedy. The band's third album *Another Mother Further* (1977) was produced by Tom Werman, noted for his work with Cheap Trick and Motley Crue, and begins with a cover of Holland-Dozier-Holland's 'Mickey's Monkey' that evokes Led Zeppelin's 'Custard Pie'. 'Piece Of The Rock' and 'Burning Love' (a song popularized by Elvis Presley) are similarly rock-heavy, while the album's kiss-off track is proudly-titled 'Hard Rock Lover'. 'Mother Factor' (1978) was more of a straight ahead funk record, but the band really rocked out on the in-concert *Live Mutha* and the next studio album *Iron Age*. Mother's Finest split in 1984, made a weak comeback record in 1989, then reasserted themselves with their heaviest work to date, 1992's *Black Radio Won't Play This Record*, an album as feisty as its title.

New York's Living Colour and Portland, Oregon's Dan Reed Network, have also faced the kind of formatting problems that inspired a title like *Black Radio Won't Play This Record*. Living Colour fluked a hit via MTV with the crunching funk metal track 'Cult Of Personality', but ultimately they were too rock for black radio stations, and too black for rock FM. Living Colour's eclecticism takes in more than plain funk and metal, but it's when Vernon Reid cranks up his guitar that this band really begins to cook.

Hawaiian-born Dan Reed is one of the most gifted songwriters of his generation, but the members of his multiracial band just don't fit the music industry's stereotypes. The Network features a black guitarist and bassist, a Japanese keyboard player and a Jewish drummer, and together they play some of the sharpest, coolest, funkiest hard rock ever conceived. Of the band's three brilliant albums, the first—eponymously-titled—is the funkiest. 'Get To You' and 'I'm So Sorry', a poignant tale of teen suicide, are reminiscent of Prince's rock cuts. On the second album, *Slam*, guitarist Brion James puts Edward Van Halen's recent performances to shame on 'Doin' The Love Thing' and the kick-ass 'Seven Sisters Road'. However, after three albums, Dan Reed still needs a hit—incredible, as he's one of the greatest writers of pop songs since the late Marc Bolan.

Funk metal isn't all black guys playing rock. In 1979, Kiss made one of the classic funk metal tracks in 'I Was Made For Loving You', a synthesis of hard rock and camp disco. Aerosmith's 'Walk This Way' was a naturally funky heavy rock number covered by black rappers Run DMC with the help of the 'Smiths' Tyler and Perry. The Beastie Boys their bratty mixed hip-hop and heavy metal on début *Licensed To Ill*, although producer and former Def Jam head Rick Rubin was the real power behind that record. Stevie Salas recalled Hendrix and the great Sly Stone with some funky power-rock on his trio's début recording *Stevie Salas Colorcode*. St Paul, formerly of Minneapolis funk legends

Flea slaps the bass for the Red Hot Chili Peppers.

the Time and the Family, fused funk and hard-edged AOR on his second solo album, *Down To The Wire*, which includes the glorious 'Stranger To Love'. Hard rockers Extreme toyed with funk on their *Porno-graffitti* album, but the Bostonians' radio-friendly records have none of the depth or credibility of the Red Hot Chili Peppers' lithe, learned funk metal. The Chilis, whose *Blood Sugar Sex Magik* album at last made them major stars, were produced in 1985 by George Clinton.

Funk metal is metal at its most celebratory. And there is no better example than the Time's 1990 comeback album *Pandemonium*. The band, co-stars of Prince's *Purple Rain* movie, are the masters of slick funk, but their guitarist Jesse Johnson is also a big hard rock fan. Two tracks on *Pandemonium*, 'Blondie' and 'Skillet', simply sizzle like that ol' skillet itself. Essential.

15

DEATH METAL

Extreme Noise Terror

DEATH METAL IS THE MOST EXTREME FORM OF MUSIC KNOWN TO MAN; HEAVY METAL AT ITS MOST VIOLENT AND INTENSE, AT ITS FASTEST, MEANEST AND UGLIEST. AS THE GENRE HAS EVOLVED, THE MUSIC HAS GROWN EVER MORE BRUTAL AND OBSCENE AS EACH NEW BAND ATTEMPTS TO TOP ALL PREVIOUS EXCESS. IN 1981,

Venom's cod-Satanic *Black Metal* seemed menacing, but in 1992, even 'In League With Satan', Venom's most terrifying number, is nothing like as shocking as Deicide's 'Oblivious To Evil' or Cannibal Corpse's 'I Cum Blood'. Just as horror films have become increasingly bloody and explicit, so has the lyrical content of death metal's nastiest exponents. Not all death metal bands are hopelessly desensitized rednecks who sit around all day drinking beer and watching gore flicks: Napalm Death are astute and politically aware, while Carcass's ghastly imagery is couched in the obscure jargon of forensic pathology, which the band gleaned from medical journals. As a whole, death metal is not for the faint of heart or the weak of stomach.

The genre's roots lie in the early Eighties. Venom are cited as a key influence by most death combos, but the phrase "death metal" was first used to describe Hellhammer, a Swiss trio who later developed into the mighty Celtic Frost. Hellhammer made just one EP, 'Apocalyptic Raids', but their name remains legendary, and not solely because the band were dubbed the worst in the world! Their music was a tortuous hybrid of Venom and Black Sabbath. In 1984, Hellhammer became Celtic Frost and the first Frost release, a mini-album titled *Morbid Tales*, is a classic, seminal death metal recording. Upon its release, Frost were proclaimed "the Black Sabbath of the Eighties", such was the power of guitarist/vocalist Tom G. Warrior's riffing. Following a second mini-album, *Emperor's Return*, Frost cut the awesome *To Mega Therion* album in 1985, on which their pounding riffs were made still heavier with the addition of thunderous horns. *To Mega Therion* was Frost's last pure death metal album. *Into The Pandemonium* (1987) bravely mixed death with all kinds of other music before 1989's *Cold Lake* foolhardily toyed with glam, losing the band's entire hardcore following. Nevertheless, Thomas Gabriel Warrior will be remembered as the eccentric genius who created some of the greatest death metal riffs of all time, and invented the "death grunt", a deep, choking exclamation beloved of all death vocalists.

Warrior is not the only bizarre character in death metal The Eighties also produced the extraordinarily named Quorthon Seth, also known as Bathory, death metal's only one-man band. Seth inhabited the wild woods of Sweden and made truly horrible heavy metal, including the legendary 'Possessed', surely the most tuneless song in recording history! However, in the Nineties has emerged the ultimate death metal madman: Glen Benton of Deicide.

Deicide are from Florida, the home of death metal. The swamplands just seem to breed these bands. Local boys Obituary, Morbid Angel, Death and Nocturnus all make music as oppressive as the Florida heat. Deicide outdo them all. Benton is an outspoken Satanist; the other three are Aryan-blond henchmen. Benton brands his forehead every day with a heated inverted crucifix and has another larger inverted cross on the outside wall of his home. He named his firstborn Daemon and wrote a song about the child's birth rights entitled 'Satan

Spawn: The Caco-Daemon'. He threatened to kill evangelist broadcaster Bob Larson on air, and his own life has been threatened by a radical British anti-vivisectionist organization, the Animal Militia, after he boasted about torturing and killing animals in a UK music paper interview.

Obituary's *Slowly We Rot* was pronounced the heaviest album ever recorded upon its release in 1989. Its noise is not as focused as Slayer's, but it is a simply gargantuan sludge. There are no actual lyrics on *Slowly We Rot*, just grim titles like 'Internal Bleeding', 'Suffocation' and 'Stinkupuss', and John Tardy's agonized subhuman roar. Many death metal vocalists use effects, principally harmonizers, to get their voices sounding like the demon inside little Linda Blair in *The Exorcist*. Tardy does not, but he's no monster, just a kid from Florida. He has some weird neighbours, though, like Morbid Angel's Trey Azagthoth (not his real name), who is prone to self-mutilation during the band's shows, and believes himself to be a vampire

and a reincarnated demon! Morbid Angel's superfast death metal is a Hell on Earth. Also from Florida are Chuck Schuldiner's Death, who cut the influential *Scream Bloody Gore* and *Leprosy* albums, but have since lapsed into slicker, formula grind.

Napalm Death are from England's second city, Birmingham. The band shot to fame with the *Scum* album, 28 tracks of primal hardcore thrash. They were tagged "the world's fastest band"—some of the songs were just two or three seconds long! By 1990 and the *Harmony Corruption* album, Napalm Death had undergone several line-up changes and had mutated into a state-of-the-art death metal band, although their lyrics remain uncommonly idealogically sound. Napalm Death's splinter groups include singer Lee Dorrian's Cathedral, who deal in pure misery and slow death, and guitarist Bill Steer's Carcass, whose downtuned and painstakingly researched gory grindcore is celebrated in such macabre titles as 'Vomited Anal Tract' and 'Cadaveric Incubator Of Endoparasites'!

17

TRADITIONAL HEAVY METAL

Heavy Habits
Die Hard

THROUGH ALL THE YEARS AND ALL THE CHANGES AND TRENDS, TRADITIONAL HEAVY METAL HAS ALWAYS REMAINED POPULAR. WHEN THE NWOBHM TURNED A SPOTLIGHT ON A CROWD OF NEW BANDS, OLD STAGERS LIKE RAINBOW, JUDAS PRIEST AND AC/DC WERE NOT THREATENED. WHEN THRASH APPEARED, IRON MAIDEN, DEF LEPPARD AND AC/DC SURVIVED. AND WHEN DEATH AND INDUSTRIAL BECAME THE NEW CUTTING EDGE OF METAL, AC/DC STILL BOOGIED ON, HAPPILY OBLIVIOUS TO IT ALL.

AC/DC headlined the UK's leading metalfest, Castle Donington's Monsters of Rock, three times between 1981 and 1991. Deep Purple have reached their twenty-fifth anniversary. Judas Priest have made 14 albums, Kiss 25.

Most traditional, classically-styled heavy metal is based on one or all of the holy trinity of Led Zeppelin, Black Sabbath and Deep Purple. Zeppelin's 'Rock And Roll', Sabbath's 'Paranoid' and Purple's 'Smoke On The Water' have been covered by a myriad bar bands over two decades.

Judas Priest and AC/DC began their careers a little later but have also proved hugely influential. No heavy metal band on the planet has not been influenced by at least one of these five bands.

Traditional heavy metal is song-based, but a great riff is also crucial. The riff is everything on 'Paranoid', 'Smoke On The Water' and any AC/DC song. Trad metal is also melodic, however powerful. Judas Priest may rattle on crazily at times, but their songs are always memorable, with a strong hook. And trad metal is fairly conservative. While critics raved about the "punk edge" on Iron Maiden's eponymous début, the band themselves were disappointed that their album didn't sound like Deep Purple's In Rock.

Iron Maiden are one of today's great traditional heavy metal bands. Everything about the band is heavy metal. The name is derived from an ancient torture instrument. Their music is charging old-school metal inspired by Priest and Purple, sung by Bruce Dickinson in the overstated manner of Deep Purple's Ian Gillan. The songs are principally tales of heroism or horror, ripping yarns like 'Phantom Of The Opera', 'Rime Of The Ancient Mariner',

'Aces High' and 'The Number Of The Beast'. Iron Maiden have a monster figurehead-cum-mascot, Eddie, a schoolboyish sense of sexuality ('Charlotte The Harlot' says it all, really) and they are occasionally unintentionally hilarious: on 'Run Silent, Run Deep', a stealthily-moving submarine is likened to "a cunning fox in the chicken's lair"!

Iron Maiden are as dependable an institution as Status Quo.

Manowar are similarly uproarious. In fact, the New Yorkers are perhaps the definitive traditional heavy metal band. They look like *Marvel* comic's superheroes, heavily muscled, dark-maned. Drummer Scott Columbus (now sadly departed) resembled, of all things, cartoon warrior Asterix's lumbering and extravagantly moustachioed sidekick Obelix! Manowar first appeared in 1982, clad in animal furs and swearing "Death to false metal!" 'Dark Avenger', a track on the début album *Battle Hymns*, featured narration by the great Orson Welles, who

Rob Halford of Judas Priest—hell bent for leather!

bellowed, in memorable fashion, "Let thee not pass, Abaddon!" Manowar entered the *Guinness Book Of Records* for playing the loudest rock gig in history and signed their UK record contract in their own blood! They made an album titled *Kings Of Metal* before setting Homer's *Iliad* to heavy metal on 'Achilles, Agony And Ecstasy In Eight Parts', the 28-minute epic centrepiece to their 1992 album *The Triumph Of Steel*.

If Manowar are the kings of metal, Judas Priest, heroes of Manowar's, are the metal gods. In Rob Halford, Priest have the ultimate heavy metal frontman. Shaven-headed and leatherbound, Halford has an unremittingly heavy metal delivery. He rants, he squeals, and he is the master of metalspeak, conjuring up song titles like 'Grinder', 'Sinner', 'Exciter' and, perhaps inevitably, 'Heavy Metal'. Halford once bid a London audience goodnight with the wonderfully tongue-in-cheek line: "I hope you've enjoyed your evening of heavy metal!" Priest albums *Unleashed In*

The East, *British Steel*, *Stained Class*, *Painkiller* and *Screaming For Vengeance* are the very epitome of no-nonsense traditional heavy metal.

Sebastian Bach of Skid Row is a huge Priest fan, and Skid Row, for all their cock rock and punk leanings, are another heavily traditional metal band, one of few such bands to break into the platinum league over recent years. Bach is still a kid, a fan, a headbanger. He couldn't believe his luck when his band—his *band!*—played at the Hammersmith Odeon (the venue immortalized by

Skid Row's wildman singer Sebastian Bach, one of the biggest mouths in metal.

Motorhead's classic live album *No Sleep 'Til Hammermsith*) in 1989, nor could he believe his luck when he got to sing Priest's 'Delivering The Goods' with Rob Halford in 1992. Skid Row's music pays homage to Priest, Kiss, AC/DC and Motorhead, but it seems Bach would happily play his favourite cover tunes all night if he could. Bach and Skid Row just love heavy metal.

Heavy metal's staunchest traditionalists have produced many of the genre's greatest moments. 'Motorcycle Man', by Barnsley's Big Teasers Saxon, is the classic expression of the free-spirited biker lifestyle beloved of metal fans. Germany's Accept are fronted by squat, cropped-haired Udo Dirkschneider, who sings like a drill sergeant and wears the army fatigues to match. The band cut some remarkable heavy metal: the grunting 'Balls To The Wall', the preposterous 'Fast As A Shark' and the somewhat homo-erotic 'London

Leatherboys'. Queensryche's precision rock is grounded in Priest, while Wolfsbane are a furious amalgam of AC/DC, Van Halen and Motorhead. Dio carried the torch for epic heavy metal, elfin singer Ronnie James Dio spinning tales of dragons, wizards and demon kings; 1983's *Holy Diver* is his masterpiece. And Ted Nugent is the traditional heavy metal wildman, a huntin', fishin' new barbarian, deadly with six strings, but even deadlier with a bowstring. The Nuge, as he is known, has recorded some outrageous heavy metal—peaking on the live albums *Intensities In Ten Cities* and *Double Live Gonzo*—and talks for as long and as loudly as he plays.

Ted Nugent once said of the term "heavy metal": "it sucks large quantities of diseased buffalo dick!"

Judas Priest, however, remain unashamedly full-on metal. Their wonderfully titled song 'Heavy Metal' is the last word on the subject: "An armour-plated raging beast that's born of steel and leather/It will survive against all odds, stampeding on forever!"

AOR
(Adult Orientated Rock)

When You've
Loved and Lost...

OVERBLOWN AND MELODRAMATIC IN THE EXTREME, CLASSIC AOR HAS THREE ESSENTIAL INGREDIENTS: A SUPERLATIVE VOCALIST, HOOK-LADEN SOFT ROCK TUNES AND A LYRICAL PREDILECTION FOR LOST LOVE AND PERSONAL TRAGEDY. ITS GREATEST EXPONENTS, THE ANGLO-AMERICAN FOREIGNER AND SAN FRANCISCO'S JOURNEY, HAVE BROKEN AS MANY HEARTS AS THEY'VE SOLD RECORDS.

AOR's combination of dramatic, bleeding-heart balladry and large-choirused rockers proves irresistible to two types of buyers: casual fans captured by radio-friendly mega hits (Foreigner's 'Waiting For A Girl Like You', REO Speedwagon's 'Keep On Loving You' or Survivor's 'Eye Of The Tiger') and the obsessive devotee tracking down the ultimate in obscurity (Only Child's eponymous release, or Icon's 'Night Of The Crime').

The AOR format developed with the expansion in US radio programming through the Seventies. The seminal pomp rockers Styx had blended progressive rock musicianship with pop sensibilities to produce perhaps the first AOR hit, 'Lady', from their 1973 release, Styx II. Boston, masterminded by studio genius Tom Scholz, were a classic example of prog rock-inspired pomp.

Producing a multi-layered wall of sound on the band's eponymous début (1976), Brad Delp's soaring voice was stacked on top of lush piano and clean guitars on the band's major hit, 'More Than A Feeling'. Scholtz's obsession with technical gimmickry led to Boston's demise; his attention to detail ensured an eight-year gap between the band's second and third releases.

Kansas, too, had prog rock roots, to the fore on their first album, Kansas (1975), but coming into line for the Leftoverture LP in 1976 This effort featured another early AOR giant, the touchingly paternal 'Carry On My Wayward Son'.

Former Santana guitarist Neil Schon founded Journey—the definitive AOR outfit—with keyboardsman Greg Rolie as Boston and Kansas were breaking big, although the band began as a jazz-fusion project. It was not until former Alien Project vocalist Steve Perry joined for 1978's Infinity that Journey began to adopt their classic AOR sound. Via Evolution (1979), Departure (1980) and the well-received live album, *Captured* (1981), Journey smoothed out the edges and, with the arrival of Jonathan Cain in place of Rolie, the band cut *Escape* in 1982. Cain's inventive keyboard wafts and sublime songwriting, Schon's aching guitar and Perry's huge-ranged and seamless voice blended into the classic American soft rock sound.

Led off by the US Number 1 single, the winsome 'Who's Crying Now', *Escape* piled it on; the pleading pathos of 'Don't Stop Believing', 'Stone In Love' and the majestic ballad 'Open Arms' ensured *Escape* spent a full two years on the Billboard charts.

Frontiers (1983) was a worthy follow-up, opening with perhaps the greatest uptempo AOR cut of all time, 'Separate Ways'. Perry's voice found new grit, even when wringing the juice from another sorrowful ballad, 'Send Her My Love'.

Raised On Radio (1986) is Journey's—and AOR's—definitive release. Not a cent of the fantastic recording budget, reputedly $1 million, was wasted; *Raised On Radio* is

verdant and diamond-hard. The reclusive Perry's solo album, *Street Talk*, is also essential listening.

AOR's most heart-warming reunion came in 1992, when English guitarist Mick Jones and masterly Italian-Amerian vocalist Lou Gramm regrouped as Foreigner. The band's combination of Free and Humble Pie-style rock tunes and unparalleled balladry has resulted in sales of over 30 million albums in the US.

Gramm had quit the band after an 11-year tenure that began with the modest *Foreigner* (1977). In 1981, Gramm cut the Mutt Lange-produced *4*, an epochal release capped by the driving 'Urgent' and the spine-tingling ballad, 'Waiting For A Girl Like You'.

Agent Provocateur topped even *4*, with Gramm's emotive, soulful voice crowning the 7 million-selling single, 'I Want To Know What Love Is', and drawing every quiver of emotion from 'Down On Love' and 'That Was Yesterday'. There wasn't a dry eye in the house.

Inside Information (1988) showed signs of weariness, but still includ-

ed two tragic ballads, 'I Don't Want To Live Without You' and 'Out Of The Blue'. While Jones dallied with new vocalist Johnny Edwards, Gramm—who'd cut two fine solo albums, *Ready Or Not* and *Long Hard Look*—formed the awesome Shadow King, whose eponymous début is a cult gem.

Perhaps the greatest pleasure for the AOR devotee is tracking down and revelling in obscure releases. Quasi-soul superstar Michael Bolton, for example, spent the greater part of the Eighties as a cult god. A former member of Blackjack, Bolton cut three classic AOR LPs, *Michael Bolton* (1983), which featured the anthemic 'Home Town Hero', *Everybody's Crazy* (1985), including the heroic 'Save Our Love', and *The Hunger* (1987), featuring 'Hot Love' and the tear-spilling ballad 'That's What Love Is All About'.

Endless arguments will erupt among AOR-heads when any list of essential cult releases holds forth; however, most would agree that no collection is complete without Night Ranger's *Seven Wishes*, Paul Sabu's

Journey, whose *Raised On Radio* (1986) is the ultimate AOR album.

Only Child's eponymous LP, Survivor's *Vital Signs*, REO Speedwagon's *Hi Infidelity* or Icon's *Night Of The Crime*.

Deeper in Cultsville, Memphis singer-songwriter John Kilzer's *Memory In The Making* is a ballsy and lean collection, matched by John Butcher's graphic *Pictures From The Front*. Diving For Pearls and Drive, She Said marry exotic names with some inspiring material, and Giant's *Last Of The Runaways* is a low key diamond, cut through with Dann Huff's spare voice.

House Of Lords, Guiffria, Balance and Glenn Burtnick all enjoyed brief moments in the sun, and two more recent underground essentials are Dare's passionate and epic *Out Of The Silence*, and From The Fire's inanely titled *Thirty Days And Dirty Nights*.

AOR's current superstar, though, is undoubtedly Richard Marx. The amply-haired American's three albums, *Richard Marx, Repeat Offender* and *Rush Street* are all classic pop rockers.

SOUTHERN ROCK

Southern by the Grace of God

IN SOUTHERN ROCK, THE GUITAR RULES; ANY SOUTHERN BAND WORTH THEIR SALT WILL HAVE TWO LEAD PLAYERS, THREE ARE PREFERABLE. DERIVED FROM ROOTSY R&B AND BRED IN LATE-NIGHT BARS, THE MUSIC IS TAGGED AFTER THE SOUTHERN STATES OF THE US, HOME TO ITS GREATEST BANDS AND FOREVER ITS GEOGRAPHICAL STRONGHOLD.

Indeed, few other musical forms glorify their origins more, or identify with them as greatly. Draped in Confederate flags, fiercely proud to be south of the Mason–Dixon line, relishing the old civil war maxim "The South will rise again", Southern Rock's biggest, baddest acts—Lynyrd Skynyrd, Blackfoot, 38. Special and Doc Holliday—leave no one doubting their roots.

Perhaps *the* seminal Southern rockers were the Allman Brothers, led by siblings Greg, and Duane—a supremely talented guitarist. Duane Allman's six-string partnership with Dickie Betts produced inspired hard boogie playing and some sublime soloing from Allman. The band's first release, *The Allman Brothers Band*, (1969) and the follow up, *Idlewild South*, (1970) produced enough strong material for the definitive live release, *At Fillmore East* (1971).

Duane Allman produced his greatest work as a member of Eric Clapton's Derek And The Dominos—his playing on the classic double album *Layla And Other Assorted Love Songs* is masterful; his is the aching slide guitar break at the climax of the LP's title track. Duane died in a motorcycle crash in 1971,

aged 24. The Allmans carried on, cutting *Eat A Peach* in 1972. Greg had a disastrous marriage to Cher, and the band faded in the late Seventies, but resurrected in 1989 for a successful twentieth anniversary tour. Their track 'Dreams' remains a classic.

Lynyrd Skynyrd, out of Jacksonville, Florida, is one of the South's true legends. The band coined the definitive triple guitar sound, produced the definitive Southern rock track, 'Freebird', and inspired myriad imitators.

Most of the band attended the same school, and adopted their name after an irascible teacher, Leonard Skinner. The spelling and pronunciation are a pun on his Southern drawl. Helpfully titling their début release *Pronounced Leh-nerd Skin-nerd*, the band produced a riot of sound that incorporated 12-bar boogie and bluesy R&B.

Pronounced's high point was the lengthy epic 'Freebird', a slide guitar-led, melodramatic paean to a free spirit. Van Zandt's rough croon and the final guitar burn-up ensured greatness. *Second Helping* included 'Sweet Home Alabama', Skynyrd's warm tribute to the South.

Lynyrd Skynyrd were devastated by the plane crash in October 1977. En route to a gig in Baton Rouge, Skynyrd's aircraft ran out of fuel and ditched in the Mississippi swamps. Ronnie Van Zandt, guitarist Steve Gaines, his sister Cassie—who sang back-ups—and a roadie, Dean Kilpatrick, died. The posthumous LP *First And Last* emerged in 1978. Spin-off band Rossington Collins enjoyed modest success, and Skynyrd reformed for a tribute tour and self-titled LP in 1990–1. Van Zandt's brother Johnnie handled vocals.

The sassy Blackfoot, like Skynyrd, hailed from Jacksonville; band leader Ricky Medlocke played drums on Skynyrd's *First And Last*. Medlocke is one of the South's great characters. Part Native American, a childhood illness that led to the removal of a lung did little to curb his holler.

Blackfoot began gigging as far back as 1968, but waited until 1975 for their vinyl début, *No Reservations*. They tasted their first national suc-

cess with the ebullient *Tomcattin* (1980), which spawned a US hit single, the lonesome 'Highway Song'.

Medlocke's songs were wild and funny. He wrote about what he knew: the road, hunting, the South. The band's albums were greatly enlivened by contributions from Medlocke's grandfather Shorty, a feisty octogenarian who blew a mean mouth organ. Shorty's spoken intro to 'Foxchase', a track from *Tomcattin*, is hilarious.

Marauder (1981) broke the band big in the UK and Europe. 'Dry County' was a Top 40 single, but it was the rattling 'Good Morning' and the moving melodrama 'Diary Of A Working Man' that hit home. Blackfoot toured hard in the UK, and recorded one of Southern Rock's classic LPs, *Highway Song Live*, at the Hammersmith Odeon in London.

Blackfoot faded after two poor releases, *Siogo* (1983) and 1984's *Vertical Smiles* (which none the less contained the superlative 'Morning Dew'), but a revamped line-up returned for a raucous show at London's Marquee in 1991, backed

up by a mini-album, *Medicine Man*.

Despite the three-piece line-up, the eschewing of the more excessive Southern traditions and their big pop success in the mid-Eighties, Texas's ZZ Top are the definitive straight Southern boogie band.

By *Eliminator* (1983), Top's distinctive, hirsute image had blended with some hi-tech, synch-driven pop rock and three stylized videos (for 'Gimme All Your Loving', 'Legs' and 'Sharp Dressed Man'), which led to world domination and a move away from Southern roots.

When Blackfoot broke through, their contemporaries followed: Bruce Brookshire's Doc Holliday keep it clean and hard, Dave Hlubeck's Molly Hatchet and Donnie (another brother of Ronnie) Van Zandt's 38. Special employ pleasingly basic bludgeon, while the now defunct Georgia Satellites failed to live up to the promise of their 1988 début.

More recently, staunch traditions have been breached by the inventive Raging Slab, who blend their Skynyrd influences with Metallica-tinged thrash!

SEATTLE GRUNGE

Sound Rites From Slicker City

GRUNGE METAL, ROOTED IN SEATTLE AND OUTLYING WASHINGTON STATE AND FUELLED BY JONATHAN PONEMAN'S STREETWISE LABEL SUBPOP, IS THE MOST SIGNIFICANT MOVEMENT IN HEAVY METAL SINCE THE CRUSHING FIRST WAVE OF THRASH REDEFINED BOUNDARIES OF SPEED AND TASTE.

The bands based around the city and its further flung, Twin Peaks-style towns read like a list of the most artistically and commercially successful new rock acts of the past year: Nirvana, Pearl Jam, Soundgarden, the Screaming Trees, Mudhoney, the Seattle supergroup Temple Of The Dog and the hottest new-comers Alice In Chains all broke out of Washington State.

As with the LA club scene of the early Eighties that spawned Motley Crue, Poison, Ratt and Guns N' Roses, Seattle is now attracting myriad wannabes—even bands from Los Angeles have relocated there. Such cynical careerism is counter-productive. Most of the local acts contend that utter boredom with their surroundings inspired both their inception and their gloom-ridden, post-punk sound.

Heavy metal legend Black Sabbath's gothic doom-mongering and casual punk nihilism fuels Seattle. Although no precise beginnings are apparent, Bob Mould's noisesters Husker Du and garage punks Green River are seminal. Inspired by a serial killer—the Green River Murderer—who claimed 30 lives and is either dead or still at large, Green River cut a semi-serious EP, 'Come On Down', in 1985. As the band became more career-minded, guitarist Steve Turner quit and was replaced by Bruce Fairweather, who joined Mark Arm (vocals), Stone Gossard (guitar), Jeff Ament (bass) and Alex Vincent (drums).

The quintet released another EP, 'Dry As A Bone', in 1987, followed by a noisefest of an album, *Rehab Doll*, in 1988. Green River split soon afterwards. Tensions came to a head at an LA club gig supporting Jane's Addiction, where Arm was pre-vented from filling the guest list with friends by Ament, who required the space for record company reps. Arm quit in disgust.

Green River's legacy is given depth by the illustrious career paths carved by Arm, Fairweather, Ament and Gossard. The music, though, is merely a signpost towards better things for the musicians and also for their producer, the influential Jack Endino.

'Dry As A Bone', 'Rehab Doll' and various extra tracks were

released as a compilation album, *Green River*, by SubPop in 1990.

Ament, Gossard and Fairweather formed Mother Love Bone immediately after the split, bringing in drummer Greg Gilmore and flamboyant frontman Andrew Wood. Wood had cut his teeth with Malfunkshun, a bizarre glam/punk combination in which Wood gave his flare for theatrics full vent.

Mother Love Bone could riff hard and grungy, but Wood wore his Bolan influences on his sleeve; the combination was both gritty and beautiful. The band cut an independently released EP, 'Shine', before signing to Polydor for their début album, *Apple* (1990).

Kicking in with the rollicking 'This Is Shangri-La', *Apple* is a heady brew of Wood's introspective, piano-led pieces and Gossard's appetite for sonic riffing. Gossard won out on sussed rockers like 'Holy Roller' and 'Star Dog Champion', both enlivened by Wood's cool vocal inflection; Wood dominated on the broody epic 'Crown Of Thorns'. *Apple* emerged

to critical acclaim, but Wood hadn't made it to the end of recording. He died of a heroin overdose, his potential only partially fulfilled.

Apple and *Shine* were re-issued in 1992 as a compilation album, *Mother Love Bone*, which includes two extra tracks, 'Lady Godiva Blues' and 'Chloe Dancer', a haunting intropiece to 'Crown Of Thorns'.

Wood's death ended Mother Love Bone. Gossard and Ament started again, hooking up with a poetic drifter, the velvet-voiced Eddie Vedder, in Pearl Jam. As Pearl Jam came together, Gossard, Ament and Vedder joined Soundgarden's Chris Cornell in recording a tribute album to Wood, *Temple Of The Dog*.

The album was cut during the day, while Pearl Jam rehearsed at night; Vedder remembers it as a uniquely

creative time. *Temple Of The Dog* is a spare, evocative set, topped by Cornell's emotional song for Wood, 'Say Hello 2 Heaven'. As Pearl Jam and Soundgarden's popularity exploded, *Temple Of The Dog* was reissued and hit platinum status.

Pearl Jam's début release *Ten*—titled after the number worn by basketball hero Mookie Blaylock—immediately set the band apart. The songs are cool, introspective and

Kurt Cobain (left) and Chris Novoselic of Nirvana.

Pearl Jam, featuring singer Eddie Vedder's brown jacket in the centre.

disturbing, finely played and capped by Vedder's husky roar. The crunch of 'Once', 'Even Flow' and 'Jeremy' is tempered by the emotive 'Black' and 'Garden'. *Ten* leans more towards the mainstream than to Seattle's noise-infested roots. Pearl Jam are a classic band.

Mudhoney, the outcome of the Arm/Turner side of the Green River split, emphasized the gap in vision within the band by adopting a sarcastic garage sound and new wave riffing. 'Every Good Boy Deserves Favour' drew Arm acclaim as Seattle's godfather, but the band's major label début, 1992's *Piece Of Cake*, was a disappointment.

The depth of Chris Cornell's songwriting for *Temple Of The Dog* was no fluke; his day job, the Black Sabbath-fired, hard-riffing Soundgarden were already cult heroes.

The band had issued a noisy début, *Ultramega OK*, through SST in 1988 and a 12-inch single, 'Flower', in May 1989 that secured a deal with A&M. Soundgarden's major-label début, *Louder Than Love*, was dense and raucous, with some biting black humour apparent in 'Big Dumb Sex'. The band broke big with their second A&M effort, the grinding *Badmotorfinger*. Soundgarden's riffing is huge, Cornell's stream-of-consciousness lyrics and gritty roar compelling. Their next release should be their watershed.

The impact of Nirvana's Geffen début, the punk-pop 'Nevermind', is discussed elsewhere—it is the most recent of the 20 classic metal releases reviewed in the albums section of this book. Nirvana are subversives in the mainstream, their leader Kurt Cobain a Johnny Rotten for the Nineties.

Screaming Trees, Tad and the Melvins are true to Seattle's noisy ideals—while the next big stars will be Alice In Chains following two off-kilter, gut-rippingly powerful albums, *Facelift* and the drug-fuelled *Dirt*. Seattle's influence has now touched Hollywood—director Cameron Crowe's feature *Singles* is about the town's musicians.

POP METAL

Metal Up
Your Charts

THE THUMPING CHORUSES, THE LOUD CLOTHES, THE HAIRCUTS… POP METAL IS NOT FOR THE SHY! A MUSICAL HYBRID COMPRISING AOR-STYLE HOOKS, WATERED-DOWN HEAVY METAL RIFFING AND POP SENSIBILITIES, POP METAL IS A BROAD CHURCH; CHEAP TRICK EVOKE THE BEATLES, DEF LEPPARD EMBODY STUDIO-BOUND HARD ROCK PERFECTION, HOT CULTISTS REDD KROSS ARE THE PARTRIDGE FAMILY DRESSED UP AS KISS, AND BRYAN ADAMS IS THE ROCK 'N' ROLLING BOY NEXT DOOR.

Adams, Leppard, Heart, Bon Jovi and Europe dominated charts in the second half of the Eighties, blurring the edges of metal and mainstream pop-rock. Pop metal is not for the po-faced. While most can produce a heart-tugging ballad (Bryan Adams's 'Heaven') or a boy-and-girl-on-the-run narrative (Bon Jovi's 'Livin' On A Prayer'), even Def Leppard's sublime, cut-glass sound is offset by some dumb jack-the-lad machismo ('Make Love Like A Man' or 'Personal Property').

Although in its considerable pomp in the mid-Eighties, pop metal has a history: Cheap Trick came together in 1972, although their eponymous début didn't emerge until five years later. With a penchant for joyous, throwaway pop, Trick's sound was engineered by flaky guitarist Rick Neilson, bassist Tom Peterson's neatly-crafted songs and Robin Zander's tuneful mid-range vox.

At Budokan (1978) became one of the top-selling US imports of all time, guaranteeing a foothold for the band. Trick followed up with the ultra-poppy 'Dream Police' (1979), but they hit the slide when Peterson quit in 1982. When he rejoined, for 1988's *Lap Of Luxury*, Cheap Trick enjoyed a US Number 1 single with 'The Flame'.

Brooklyn-born vocalist Pat Benatar also married hard-edged guitaring (from her husband Neil Geraldo) with classic pop choruses

Def Leppard on stage with the late Steve Clark (left).

to score big in 1981 with her *Precious Time* LP. Benatar cut against the grain with her hit 'Sex As A Weapon', a clever snipe at deep-rooted sexism in rock, and her refusal to indulge in soft-focus flaunting lent credibility. Pop metal,

Bon Jovi during their marathon *Slippery When Wet* tour in 1986.

though, is a fickle master; Benatar was history by the late Eighties.

Seattle's Heart, fronted by the Wilson sisters, Ann (vocals) and Nancy (guitar), flitted between Led Zep-inspired rifferama ('Barracuda') and brash pop rock ('Crazy On You'). The band's early career was patchy, but 1985's *Heart* turned the tables, a crafty blend of ethereal key-

boards, glassy guitars and rich vocals. The singles 'What About Love' and 'These Dreams' ensured success.

New Jersey's Bon Jovi embraced pop metal in its purest form; they enjoy both a pop heart-throb reputation and a hardcore metal following. Led by the square-jawed Italian-American Jon Bon Jovi, the band's self-titled 1984 début included the surprise hit 'Runaway', but the lame follow-up, *7,800 Fahrenheit*, meant Bon Jovi were starting from scratch with 1986's *Slippery When Wet*. With the lead-off singles, 'You Give Love A Bad Name' and 'Livin' On A Prayer', co-written with pop metal guru Desmond Child (also noted for his work with Cher and Aerosmith), *Slippery When Wet* was un-stoppable. Jon's good looks melted hearts and *Slippery* melt-ed charts, shifting a cool 14 million units despite being laden

with lumpen fillers like 'Let It Rock' and 'I'd Die For You'. The follow-up, *New Jersey*, repeated the formula with the 'Bad Medicine' single, but elsewhere bore the tiresome hallmarks of Jon's Springsteen obsession. As marathon tours put the band in the supertax bracket, Jon cut a solo album, *Blaze Of Glory*, which indulged his cowboy fetish—it was the soundtrack to the western *Young Guns II*. For a time, its success seemed to have marked the end of Bon Jovi, but the band buried the hatchet for 1992's *Keep The Faith*, a more mature work, for sure.

The hare-brained Swedes Europe matched Bon Jovi hit for hit in 1986. In the flaxen-haired Joey Tempest they had a frontman as gorgeous as Jon Bon Jovi, and in 'The Final Countdown' they had a worldwide hit. 'The Final Countdown' was a wonderfully silly cod-sci fi anthem led off by a mind-numbing, parping keyboard riff and Tempest's hammy vocals. Euro-metal in every respect, Europe followed up with the brain-dead but infectious 'Rock The Night' and the hilarious Red Indian romp

'Cherokee'. The lacrimose ballad 'Carrie' also enjoyed chart action. The follow-up, *Out Of This World* (1988) was a disappointment from which Europe—trapped in the credibility gap—have been unable to recover.

Before Bryan Adams broke all records with his tearful 1991 ballad '(Everything I Do) I Do It For You', he'd carved a reputation as a songwriter of craft and quality and a gritty live performer. His 1985 release, *Reckless*, remains his zenith. 'Run To You' showcased tough guitars with an infectious tune, and the nostalgic 'Summer Of '69', the power-ballad 'Heaven' and a duet with Tina Turner, 'It's Only Love', won him a massive following. Adams lost ground with the introspective and underrated *Into The Fire* (1987), but the Mutt Lange-produced *Waking Up The Neighbours* (1991) has topped even *Reckless* in terms of commercial success.

Producer Lange, though, is still best known as Def Leppard's "sixth member", his painstaking, perfectionist approach honing their classic

hard rock tunes into state-of-the-art pop metal. *Pyromania* (1983) was topped by *Hysteria* (1987); both are essential releases.

Pop metal is a fickle and transient genre; bands can dominate overnight and disappear just as quickly—fans grow up while follow-up albums are being cut. The all-encompassing power of radio play in the US breaks hearts and snaps careers. White Lion hit big with *Pride* (1987), but split after the follow-ups, *Big Game* and *Mane Attraction* flopped by comparison. Similarly the John Waite-fronted Bad English enjoyed success with 'When I See You Smile' from their self-titled début, but were gone a year later. Warrant, after two big, dumb successes with *Dirty Rotten Filthy Stinking Rich* and *Cherry Pie*, have gone for the metal following with their balls-out, non-commercial third LP, *Dog Eat Dog*.

Mr Big, Chicago's cool Enuff Z'nuff and Scarborough's Little Angels have continued the pop metal theme; all would trade hit singles for long-term, album-based success—pop metal's nirvana.

ROCK 'N' ROLL

R 'N' R—Raunch
'n' Rebellion

NOT, OF COURSE, THE ROCK 'N' ROLL OF ELVIS AND BILL HALEY, BUT A GUITAR-FUELLED AMALGAM OF SASSY ROCK GROOVES AND COOL TUNES CURRENTLY EPITOMIZED BY GUNS N' ROSES'S STREET-PUNK FIRE AND THE BLACK CROWES' CLASSIC RETRO TUNES.

Ultimately rooted in black blues and R&B, and defined by British legends the Rolling Stones, Free, Mott The Hoople and Humble Pie, rock 'n' roll is now a cosy blanket term to drape on cussed survivors like Aerosmith, US trash exponents like Faster Pussycat and Ratt, and even uninspired and dumb hard rockers like Love/Hate and Slaughter.

Guns N' Roses, the hard rock band of the past half-decade, cut it all loose with *Appetite For Destruction*, their lethal 1987 début (see the classic albums and legends sections). While many could claim to stick closer to the musical formula—Guns N' Roses were as punk as they were rock—the quintet lived and breathed the wild spirit of rock 'n' roll; they drank, cursed and rocked their way to megastardom, they were every parent's nightmare. Even as their lengthy *Use Your Illusion* brace of LPs showed the band's ambition to embrace a wider and more sophisticated mix of styles, their behaviour remained brattishly dreadful, and the band remain the inspiration for a generation.

Georgia's Black Crowes stay closest to the classic, rootsy Seventies rock 'n' roll sound; Humble Pie and Faces grooves are embellished with cool riffing and Chris Robinson's wonderful, Rod Stewart-redolent vocals. Live, they are intense and inspired, on record, they're cool and loose; the Black Crowes are the best rock 'n' roll band in the world today. Formed by Chris and his introspective, guitar-playing younger brother Rich, under the moniker Mr Crowe's Garden, the Crowes were signed by Rick Rubin's streetwise rock label Def American in 1989, and cut their George Drakoulias-produced début a year later.

Shake Your Money Maker was a sensation. The Robinson brothers' songwriting was mature beyond their years, incorporating Motown and soul sounds—the title is a James Brown line—as well as their more apparent influences. Their cover of Otis Redding's 'Hard To Handle' is both respectful and joyously hardedged, while some of their originals, the cool 'Jealous Again' and the far tougher 'Twice As Hard', bear comparison.

With an appetite for touring as great as their appetite for music, the Black Crowes were big league overnight. The inevitable tensions stoked up by a 2-year road schedule resulted in second guitarist Jeff Cease quitting at the end of the tour. After flirting with departed Guns N' Roses guitarist Izzy Stradlin', Cease's eventual replacement was an inspired choice, Marc Ford, who had led fiery retro-rockers Burning Tree before hooking up with his close friend Chris Robinson.

The band cut the follow-up to *Shake Your Money Maker*, 1992's *The Southern Harmony And Musical Companion,* in 8 days to ensure a live vibe and constant groove. Enlivened by Ford's intense and dark soloing, *Companion* is a blissful rock classic, shot through with fine songs, lush piano and female harmonies, and over all Chris Robinson's beautiful, soulful voice.

The Crowes' UK equivalents, Newcastle rock 'n' rollers the Quireboys, are stilted and contrived by comparison.

Aerosmith enter the new decade as rock 'n' roll's elder statesmen, bolstered by the mystique acquired as they came through a musically barren spell that coincided with heavy drug use to regain the peak of popularity they achieved with their classic releases *Toys In The Attic* (1975) and *Rocks* (1976). *Permanent Vacation* (1987) retained the band's raunch and groove, but added some diamond-hard and lewd contemporary rockers— 'Dude (Looks Like A Lady)' and 'Heart's Done Time'. With the slick and saucy *Pump* as a follow-up, Aerosmith remain a major act in their third decade.

In the hot LA club scene of the Eighties, the defining edges of glam and rock 'n' roll blurred; Poison and Motley Crue would lay claim to a rock 'n' roll sound despite the big hair and bad make-up. The less successful wannabes—Faster Pussycat and the super-dumb Ratt— tried hard to keep up. Cult glam gods Hanoi Rocks are another genre-crossing case in point. The sadly-defunct Broken Homes are worthy of a mention here; their third album, *Wing And A Prayer,* is fine, hard-driving, commercial rock 'n' roll.

British rock 'n' roll has failed to ring true— cowboy boots and sleaze on a rainy night in a dingy UK city are hard to carry off. The world-weary Dogs D'Amour, led by the dishevelled Tyla, enjoyed some UK success, but were a mere drop in the mad ocean of LA clubland.

The Seventies, though, remain a golden memory. Ian Hunter's Mott The Hoople dominated the early part of the decade. Humble Pie, imbued by Steve Marriott's husky rasp, are cited by the Black Crowes' Chris Robinson as a major influence. Free, and later Bad Company, defined the loose groove and sublime songwriting that are still unmatched. If *Tons Of Sobs* (1969), *Fire And Water* (1970) or *Straight Shooter* (1975) were cut today, the competition would be brushed aside.

America remains rock 'n' roll nirvana, although the LA scene has diminished in influence with the rise of Seattle-inspired heavy riffing grunge. The press championed Love/Hate could make no impression in the US with their raucous, naive romps, and Slaughter slipped away, unable to follow the remarkably crass hit 'Up All Night'.

AC/DC

See separate entry in the Legends section.

BRYAN ADAMS

For a man who began his career as a member of Sweeny Todd, it's appropriate that square-jawed Canadian soft-rocker Bryan Adams's breakthrough album was titled *Cuts Like A Knife*. The rumbustious *Cuts* (1983) was Adams's third solo release; his eponymous début (1980) and *You Want It, You Got It* (1981), blue-collar rockers both, broke ground in his domestic market. *Cuts*, and stand-out track 'This Time', a consummate AOR hookfest, opened up North America.

Adams's songwriting partnership with Jim Vallance matured to devastating effect on 1985's *Reckless*, a bone-fide AOR/pop rock classic. The hard-driving 'Run To You', an emotive power-ballad, 'Heaven', and a duet with Tina Turner, 'It's Only Love', powered worldwide sales of *Reckless* through 4 million. Adams's "boy-next-door" good looks made crossover pop success easy. Strangely, the LP's best tune, 'Summer Of '69', was not a major hit, but remains a highpoint of Adams's raucous live set.

As a commercial follow-up to *Reckless*, *Into The Fire* (1987) flopped. Introspective where *Reckless* was brazen, *Into The Fire*'s best moments are the melancholic title track and the ballsy 'Hearts On Fire'.

Adams teamed up with Def Leppard/Foreigner production guru Robert John "Mutt" Lange to re-establish himself. Lange's musical signatures—multi-tracked vocal harmonies and diamond-hard guitars—are all over *Waking Up The Neighbours* (1991). *Waking* is Bryan Adams sings Def Leppard, an irresistible chart combination. Led by the maudlin ballad 'Everything I Do (I Do

It For You)', a soundtrack piece for the hit movie *Robin Hood, Prince Of Thieves* that topped charts worldwide and spent a record-breaking 16 weeks astride the UK Top 40, *Waking* made Adams a stadium-filling superstar, at the cost of his musical identity.

AEROSMITH

See separate entry in the Legends section.

ALICE IN CHAINS

Late-breakers from the pre-eminent Seattle grunge scene of the early Nineties, Alice In Chains are emergent superstars. The band's sound, built around dense guitars and Layne Staley's hypnotic roar, is more sophisticated than Nirvana, more direct than Pearl Jam, less primitive than Soundgarden, and still possesses the dark underbelly that all three evoke so well.

Facelift (1990) was an impressive début, spacey in parts, spare in others, and an acoustic EP, 'Sap', marked a degree of creative depth.

The band's admitted dalliance with hard drugs provides *Dirt* (1992) with a nightmarish quality and a dangerous lyrical edge. Graphic and visceral, *Dirt* has sold heavily throughout the USA and Europe.

Alice In Chains are a band on the edge, in more ways than one.

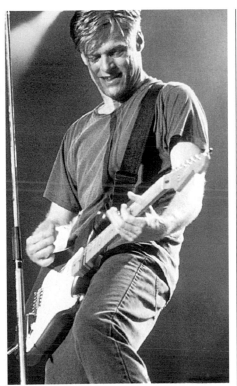

Bryan Adams: the Canadian hard rocker's maudlin '(Everything I Do) I Do It For You' topped the UK chart for 4 months!

THE ALMIGHTY

The Almighty are fiery British rockers, the natural successors to Motorhead. Led by flame-haired vocalist/rhythm guitarist Ricky Warwick, formerly of New Model Army, the Almighty trade heavily on aggression. The inspirational force of their early live shows overpowered some workaday songwriting, but when the Almighty got that right, as with the seminal 'Full Force Loving Machine', they proved a ferocious extension to the tradition of British Power Metal.

Their 1989 début, *Blood, Fire And Love*, is a display of force over finesse, and, backed by a road-melting live schedule, it broke the band in the UK. A live EP from the shows, 'Blood, Fire And Live' (1990) does little to capture the band's noisy spirit.

The second album proper, *Soul Destruction*, cemented their reputation and promised much for the future, especially on the epic 'Bandaged Knees'. Inter-band wrangling led to the departure of guitarist Tantrum, who was replaced by former Alice Cooper session man Pete Freezin. Freezin leant the band an even harsher edge at their landmark opening slot at the UK Donington Monsters of Rock Festival in 1992. The band's fourth release, *Powertrippin*, will be the watershed.

✝✝✝

ANTHRAX

The hard riffing orthodoxy of Anthrax's début album, directly titled *Fistful Of Metal* (1983), was an unlikely herald for what was to follow. The quintet's forceful speed metal carved them a place in thrash's big four along with Metallica, Megadeth and the savage Slayer.

The band were pulled together in New York by guitarist Scott Ian and bassist Dan Lilker. They ground through myriad line-ups before settling with vocalist Neil Turbin and drummer Charlie Benante. Work on *Fistful* began after the band signed with thrash entrepreneur Johnny Z's then fledgling Megaforce label (which also gave breaks to Metallica and King's X).

Internal wrangles led to the departure of Turbin and Lilker in 1984. Lilker went on to form Nuclear Assault,

Anthrax guitarist Dan Spitz on the left, bassist Frank Bellow and the now departed singer Joey Belladonna.

and later Brutal Truth. Anthrax replaced the pair with singer Joey Belladonna and guitarist Dan Spitz for the breakthrough release *Spreading The Disease* (1984). A carnival of speedy riffage, *Spreading* sat well with other key releases at the beginning of thrash's golden era, although *Spreading*'s naive brutality has failed the test of time.

Adopting a cartoonish image and skateboard-inspired fashions, Anthrax's toytown looks and ill-advised Rap parody 'I'm The Man' detracted from some excellent work. *Among The Living* (1987) threw up a hit single, the meaty 'I Am The Law', and1990's *Persistence Of Time* included an unlikely and biting cover of Joe Jackson's pseudo-jazz tune 'Got The Time'.

Scott Ian's love of rap and hip-hop music resulted in a fine collaboration with Public Enemy, 'Bring The Noise', but also made apparent the division between the band and Joey Belladonna, who favoured a more mainstream rock 'n' roll direction.

In 1992, Anthrax replaced Belladonna with former Armored Saint howler John Bush, toned down their clownish image and cut a new LP, *The Sound Of White Noise,* without doubt their finest yet.

BAD COMPANY

With the ragged dissolution of Britain's greatest blues rockers, Free, their sublimely talented vocalist Paul Rodgers and drummer Simon Kirke put together Bad Company along similar, easy-grooving and evocative lines.

Complemented by guitarist Mick Ralphs and bassist Boz Burrell, Bad Company picked up Free's vibe for their eponymous début (1974), a tight set that broke through on the back of a worldwide hit, 'Can't Get Enough'.

Once in the slot, Bad Company were unshakeable, if at times leaden-footed. *Straight Shooter* (1974) threw up another gem, the hazy 'Feel Like Makin' Love', and at times, the band matched Free's effortless grace.

Successive releases *Run With The Pack* (1976), *Burnin' Sky* (1977) and *Desolation Angels* (1979), coupled with a fruitful association with Led Zeppelin's manager Peter Grant, marked Bad Company out as major arena stars, their ability to cut one or two classic tracks per album overcoming a general propensity towards repetition. Rodgers's soulful voice effortlessly wrenched ordinary tunes on to higher ground.

The band split in 1982. A late Eighties reunion *sans* Rodgers and with the journeyman Brian Howe in his stead met with steady success on the US oldies' circuit.

THE BLACK CROWES

The Black Crowes are cool and sassy, a sweet rock 'n' roll band in the grand tradition of Humble Pie and the Rolling Stones. Infused with Chris Robinson's inspiring voice, the Crowes write great songs with great passion. The band was formed in Atlanta, Georgia, by Chris, guitarist brother Rich, fellow six-stringer Jeff Cease, drummer Steve Gorman and bassist Johnny Colt from

The Black Crowes at the time of the release of their first album, *Shake Your Money Maker*, with former guitarist Jeff Cease (left).

the ashes of the Robinsons' previous outfit, Mr Crowe's Garden.

Their début album *Shake Your Money Maker* (1990) took off like a rocket. It was part heavy groove ('Twice As Hard', 'Jealous Again', 'Stare It Cold') and part mellow soul ('She Talks To Angels', 'Seeing Things'). By the time *The Southern Harmony And Musical Companion* was cut in 8 days and released in 1992, the Black Crowes were hardened road warriors with an attitude as genuine as their music.

The Southern Harmony And Musical Companion is full of guts and spirit, superbly played and given a dark edge by Marc Ford's blistering guitar work. Ford had replaced Cease for the making of the second LP, stepping out of his previous band, the inspired retro-rockers Burning Tree, to renew a long-standing friendship with Chris Robinson.

Signed by Rick Rubin to his streetwise Def American label, the Crowes encapsulate much of what the bearded guru stands for, real music played with passion and soul, unyielding in the face of current trends.

BLACK SABBATH

See separate entry in the Legends section.

BLUE CHEER

Grim and unsubtle, grizzled bikers Blue Cheer are often credited with producing one of the first metal sounds, an overdriven semi-psychedelic racket untroubled by good songs. The trio (guitarist/vocalist Leigh Stephens, bassist Dick Peterson and drummer Paul Whaley) cut *Vincibus Eruptum* in 1968, an album seminal in its volume and lack of finesse.

BLUE OYSTER CULT

Resolutely mysterious and once known as Soft White Underbelly, Blue Oyster Cult's sonic riffage is coupled with some grand conceptual ideas that have kept the quintet buoyant—with varying degrees of success—since their self-titled début album was issued in 1971.

Mixing vague Zeppelin-isms with an early blues influence, BOC built a strong following via *Tyranny And Mutation* (1973), and *Secret Treaties* (1974), which featured 'Career Of Evil', a tune penned by guitarist/keyboardist Alan Lanier's then girlfriend Patti Smith. Smith also contributed vocals to *Agents Of Fortune* (1976), an album that included BOC's greatest song, the hypnotic epic 'Don't Fear The Reaper', a US and UK hit single.

Band leader Donald Roeser adopted an unlikely second persona, "Buck Dharma", and the band enjoyed renewed interest in 1980 when the aptly titled *Cultosaurus Erectus* stood proud at Number 12 in the UK albums charts, their biggest hit to date.

Drummer Albert Bouchard quit BOC before the 1988 release of *Imaginos,* a convoluted and cumbersome concept album, but then claimed to be the sole creative influence behind the LP and threatened to take action against the remaining members. Intriguingly, the band returned, *sans* Bouchard, for some well-received film soundtrack work.

BODY COUNT

Acid-tongued rapper Ice-T split the US with 'Cop Killer', an incendiary track from his rap/metal crossover band Body Count's eponymous first LP.

'Cop Killer' glorified violence against authority at a time when the US was blighted by racial tension in its larger cities—Rodney King had been beaten into infamy by the LAPD. Ice-T claimed that Body Count were a voice for and from the ghettos, and anyway, the song was delivered tongue-in-cheek. However, even President George Bush spoke out publicly against the song and, amid raging debate, Ice-T ordered that 'Cop Killer' be removed from future pressings of the album after threats were made against personnel from his label, Warner Bros.

Body Count bears out Ice-T's claims of tongue-in-cheek lyricism. 'KKK Bitch' and 'Evil Dick' are nasty rockers, unsubtle and mysogynistic, but they hardly undermine the fabric of society. Body Count are not the revolutionaries they've been portrayed, and ultimately lack the creative momentum to break down barriers.

Ice-T split with Warner Bros in 1993 in the wake of the 'Cop Killer' row.

BON JOVI

With giant pop metal hooks, pin-up boy looks and one eyed determination, Bon Jovi made world domination look simple. Their marriage of teen-appeal image and credible rock musicianship ensured the New Jersey quintet could cover all bases—fickle singles' chart success and a hardcore, durable heavy metal following.

All-American teenager Jon Bongiovi (later anglicized to Bon Jovi) was relentless in pursuit of success. Some

high-quality demos he cut while sweeping up in a recording studio led to a long-term deal with Polygram.

Putting together a band—Tico Torres (drums), David Bryan (keyboards) and Alec John Such (bass)—around his writing partnership with elegant guitarist Richie Sambora, Bon Jovi's self-titled début album (1984) included an AOR radio success, 'Runaway', and gained the band acclaim in the metal press. When it seemed that even their unfeasible poodle-perms would be no barrier to success, Bon Jovi's second effort, the wayward *7,800 Fahrenheit*, failed to deliver.

Thus, when *Slippery When Wet* was cut and released in 1986, eventual worldwide sales of 14 million units seemed unlikely. However, the hard-edged and hooky pop metal classics 'You Give Love A Bad Name' and 'Livin' On A Prayer', co-written with cult AOR artist Desmond Child, were made for US radio; backed with a ruthless touring schedule and those heart-fluttering smiles, Bon Jovi could not fail. A follow-up, *New Jersey* (1988), was cut from the same cloth. For 'You Give Love' read 'Bad Medicine'.

Where *New Jersey* gave reign to Jon Bon Jovi's Springsteen fetish, his cowboy dreams were fulfilled by the monumental success of his cheesy *Young Guns II* soundtrack solo album, *Blaze Of Glory*. When Sambora cut his own solo effort, *Stranger In This Town*, the press speculated that the band were finished. However, *Keep The Faith* (1993) gave lie to the rumours. Bon Jovi returned with their least obvious—and therefore most artistically satisfying—release to date.

BOSTON

Boston epitomized faceless corporate rock; wonderfully crafted yet soulless studio artistry. Led by studio genius Tom Scholz, Boston's albums were painstakingly pieced together at almost unendurable length. The upside of such grim determination was 'More Than A Feeling', the diamond-hard AOR gem from the band's eponymous début (1976) which still enjoys radio play.

Boston and its follow-up *Don't Look Back* (1978) proved huge hits, however, but Scholz's 8-year (!) quest for recorded perfection on *Third Stage* (1986) effortlessly quashed the band's momentum.

BUDGIE

This band's apologetically humorous name encapsulated their lack of ambition; had they been American and called, say, Vulture, Budgie's basic, memorable riffing over some ten albums would have ensured more than minor cult success. 'Breadfan' and 'Turn To Stone' are classic songs.

Budgie are now best known for having their songs covered by Metallica, who acknowledge the Welsh rockers as a major influence.

BURNING TREE

A classic and underrated retro-rock trio, Burning Tree released one moody, self-titled LP (1990) for the Epic label before they split. Bassist Doni Gray and drummer Mark Dutton went on to work with an early incarnation of former Guns N' Roses guitarist Izzy Stradlin's solo band, while guitarist/vocalist Marc Ford renewed his friendship with Chris Robinson in the Black Crowes.

Named after a street in which Ford's girlfriend lived, Burning Tree mixed blistering guitars with psychedelic rock riffs and beautifully winsome tunes. 'Mistreated Lover' is misty with rock history, 'Crush' is memorably hooky, and 'Baker's Song' is an unforgettable ballad. Burning Tree choked on a lack of enthusiasm from a record company for one of its best products.

CELTIC FROST

Heavy metal gets no more bizarre than Celtic Frost, a seminal death metal quartet who have embraced glam rock and hip-hop. Inspired by the avant-garde genius of quirky frontman Thomas Gabriel Warrior, Frost's fourth LP, *Into The Pandemonium* (1987), is an essential death metal work.

Warrior put Frost together in his native Switzerland from the remnants of Hellhammer, an almost unlistenably extreme band. *Morbid Tales* (1984), *Emperor's Return* (1985) and the awe-inspiring *To Mega Therion* (1985) broke ground in the extremes of brutality; Warrior coined his unique "death grunt" along the way.

With cult status wrapped up, Frost proceeded to lose their entire fan base with *Cold Lake* (1989). Warrior emerged with hair teased into a gothic bird's nest and liberally applied lipgloss having cut a glam rock album! A return to death metal roots, *Vanity/Nemesis* (1990) barely repaired the damage.

Warrior has relocated to Texas and plans to cut another extreme metal album.

Celtic Frost in 1991 with, from the left, Tom G. Warrior, Stephen Priestly, Curt Victor Bryant and Martin Eric Ain.

CHEAP TRICK

With *At Budokan*, US pop metallers Cheap Trick defined a classic sound, Robin Zander's Beatles-style vocal harmonies set on Rick Nielsen's powerchording guitars. The album, recorded live at Japan's premier concert hall, broke the band throughout the US.

Following the departure of bassist Tom Petersen, Cheap Trick fell into a decline which was only arrested by the four-stringer's return for 1988's *Lap Of Luxury*, a fulsome set topped by the hit ballad, 'The Flame'.

CINDERELLA

Cinderella started out as humble as their fairy-tale namesake, then large-scale success induced an ill-fated conversion to unconvincing blues rock.

The band's début, *Night Songs*, was neatly trashy, but lent substance by Tom Kiefer's gutteral howl and ballsy guitaring. The follow-up, *Long Cold Winter*, worked best when the band pursued their paint-by-numbers hard raunch à la 'Gypsy Road', and fell short when Kiefer's blues fetishes were given their head.

With two million-selling albums behind them, Cinderella lost sight of their major assets—the ability to perform trim glam metal with gusto—and instead produced the turgid *Heartbreak Station*, an album which set their career into decline.

Cinderella. Clockwise from left: Eric Brittingham, Jeff La Bar, Tom Kiefer and Fred Coury (now with Arcade).

ALICE COOPER

In a career that has included in excess of 20 albums, Alice Cooper (née Vincent Furnier) remains best known and best loved for his schlock horror stage extravaganzas—part magical illusion, part grisly Grand Guignol. Plastered in eyeliner and sheathed in leather, Cooper played ring-master to some outlandish stage stunts. Ghouls were hung, women whipped, babies speared and Cooper himself was convincingly guillotined.

Born in Detriot, Cooper became a staple of the Los Angeles club scene in the late Sixties. As his stage shows and outlandish press claims provoked public outrage, Cooper rode on the crest of some brash pop metal; 'I'm Eighteen', 'No More Mr Nice Guy', 'Elected' and the ubiquitous anti-parent anthem 'School's Out'.

A series of huge albums, *Killer* (1971), *Billion Dollar Babies* (1973), *Muscle Of Love* (1974) and his best, *Welcome To My Nightmare* (1975), marked the path to an infamy in which Cooper revelled.

As he declined into alcoholism, Cooper's days appeared numbered, but he achieved an unlikely come-back with *Trash* (1989), a hard pop album which lent on established tunesmiths like Desmond Child. Cooper's reputation has encouraged contributions from modern era stars (Guns N' Roses's guitarist Slash, for example)

An ageing Alice Cooper, who defeated alcoholism to make an incredible comeback with *Trash*.
....

and the man, still unconvincingly plastered in eyeliner, has gleefully accepted his second chance. A cameo appearance in the hit movie *Wayne's World* and a carbon copy of *Trash*, *Hey Stoopid*, completed a Lazarus-style return.

THE CULT

For two iron men of rock, the Cult's mainstays Ian Astbury (vocals) and Billy Duffy (guitar) enjoyed—or endured—a bizarre early career as gothic punk heroes. Caked in black eyeliner and paisley scarves, the band attracted a strong UK underground following as Southern Death Cult, before dropping first the "Southern" and later "Death" from the name.

Trimmed down to the Cult and with the greater gothic excesses chipped away from their inspirational riffing, the band issued their Steve Brown-produced second LP, *Love*, in 1985. Brown retained the exotic qualities of the Cult's early work, but allowed Duffy's fiery riffs their head. With Astbury burgeoning into a card-carrying rock god, shaking his raven-black mane and unveiling a convincing metallic howl, 'Rain', 'Love' and the epic 'She Sells Sanctuary'—the band's first hit—established the Cult as potent, full-bore rockers.

Pledging their allegiance to the legacy of Led Zeppelin and AC/DC, the Cult scrapped the early Steve Brown recordings of their next album, *Electric*, for lacking directness and began work with Def American guru Rick Rubin.

Electric (1987) was a revelation, a high-octane mix of power riffage, explosive rhythms and great songs. Tracks like 'Li'l Devil', the AC/DC-flavoured 'Wild Flower' and the brazen 'Love Removal Machine' elevated the Cult to arena status throughout Europe. *Sonic Temple* (1989), produced by metalheaded knob-twiddler Bob Rock, was another ripsnorting set, with the gutsy 'Fire Woman' and 'Sun King' offset by the quite beautiful 'Edie (Ciao Baby)', a tune inspired by the doomed actress Edie Sedgwick.

Ceremony (1991) knocked the Cult back a step. Astbury's wish to remain in full-on metal mode overpowered Duffy's desire to move along, and Duffy was quick to point out his displeasure with the set, which none the less produced the hard-grooving 'Wild Hearted Son'. Astbury used the album to highlight another of his causes, the plight of the Native American.

A neat compilation, *Pure Cult* (1993) put the band back on an even keel. Reuniting with Rick Rubin for a new track, the industrially-flavoured 'The Witch', for inclusion on *Pure Cult*, the band look set to reinvent themselves again.

DANZIG

Morbid and gothic, Danzig is a vehicle—most likely a hearse—for musclebound former Samhain and Misfits frontman Glenn Danzig.

Danzig veer between the compelling and the comic. When they get it right, as with 'Mother' or 'The Hunter' from their eponymous début (1988), Danzig are a crushing, Doors-inspired force. When it goes wrong, Glenn Danzig's Fifties rock 'n' roller croon and po-faced posturing are more comic than chilling, earning him the disparaging nickname "the Evil Elvis".

Espousing a cod-Satanic philosophy tacked onto some dark riff-fests, the success of the band's second release, *Danzig II: Lucifuge,* depends much on how far the fan is prepared to suspend reality and tread in grim Glenn's footprints. *How The Gods Kill* (1992) was more fodder for the faithful.

Former Misfits/Samhain frontman Glenn Danzig, nicknamed "the Evil Elvis", or "the Satanic Fonz"!

DEEP PURPLE

In their triumphant Seventies dogdays, Deep Purple were a hot component in heavy metal's ruling triumverate. If Led Zeppelin were the blues on an epic scale, and Black Sabbath the brute and elemental force, Deep Purple were the hard driving, overblown classicists. Their sound—led off by Ritchie Blackmore's lean, tough riffs and Jon Lord's ghostly Hammond organ—had both muscularity and finesse. Purple's reputation would ride higher today but for a series of spectacularly horrid reformations which continue to date.

A spluttering start was smoothed out when Deep Purple tied down their definitive "Mark II" line-up—Ritchie Blackmore (guitar), Ian Paice (drums), Roger Glover (bass), Jon Lord (keyboards) and Ian Gillan (vocals)—for the *In Rock* LP (1970, and reassessed elsewhere). Gillan's lung busting wail was Purple's missing link. Alternately whispering like a babe and howling like a whipped cat, Gillan turned in some mesmerizing performances, particularly on the epic 'Child In Time'.

Fireball (1971) and *Machine Head* (1971 and featuring the band's—perhaps even heavy metal's—best known riff 'Smoke On The Water') cemented Deep Purple's status; 'Fireball', 'Highway Star' and 'Space Truckin'' are classic tracks.

Made In Japan (1972) celebrated the band's lengthy live shows. Fortunately, it didn't reflect growing tensions within the line-up. Gillan left in 1973, to be replaced by a former shop assistant from Redcar, UK, David Coverdale. Trapeze's talented but wayward bassist/vocalist Glenn Hughes was in too, in place of Roger Glover.

Burn (1974) was immediately cohesive, the title track and Coverdale's vocal extravanza 'Mistreated' made a forceful case for the new line-up.

However, *Stormbringer* (1974) gave some vent to a funkier direction that the overlord Blackmore disliked. He quit in a fit of pique to form Rainbow (see separate entry). His replacement was Tommy Bolin, a wonderful player who found the trappings of stardom too large a burden. *Come Taste The Band* (1975) was low-key in comparison to Purple's strident past. Coverdale quit in 1976 and Purple crumbled. Bolin was dead from drug abuse by the following year.

The excitement surrounding the "Mark II" line-up's reformation in 1984 soon dissipated after *Perfect Strangers* and *House Of Blue Light* (1987). Purple's creativity was spent, their egos, unfortunately, still rampant. Gillan's second tenure ended after bitter rowing with Ritchie Blackmore. Ludicrously, Blackmore bought in his Rainbow sidekick Joe Lynn Turner, thus destroying the remnants of Purple's credibility.

Gillan's decision to rejoin again in 1993 was met with the apathy its cynicism fully deserved.

DEF LEPPARD

See separate entry in the Legends section.

Deep Purple *circa* 1976 with, clockwise from left, Tommy Bolin, Ian Paice, David Coverdale, Jon Lord and Glenn Hughes.

DEICIDE

Floridian black metallers Deicide are fronted by heavy metal's newest nutter, the gleefully unrepentant Satanist Glen Benton.

In a brief but colourful career, Benton has wreaked mayhem and outrage by giving vent to his apparent devotion to the Devil. As Deicide rose from the buzzing Florida death metal scene, Benton marked out himself and his band by claiming that they would all commit suicide at the age of 33, having proven that they could outlive Jesus Christ, who was thought to have been 32 when he died on the cross!

Benton then provoked Christian fundamentalist fury with several appearances on US radio host Bob Larson's networked show, baiting listeners by approving of Satanic sacrifices. Upon becoming a father, he named his firstborn son Daemon, and penned a song, 'Satan Spawn: The Caco-Daemon', for the infant on Deicide's second LP, the noisy but uninventive *Legion* (1992).

The band's first UK tour, in 1990, was abandoned halfway through when Benton was set upon by less-than-gullible British fans, who stole his favourite bass guitar. Benton boasted of torturing small animals for fun to the press, and a UK animal rights group, the Animal Militia, vowed revenge. Deicide's two English shows in 1992 went ahead with heavy security in operation.

DIAMOND HEAD

Following a reformation in 1993, Diamond Head at last have a chance to fulfil their outrageous potential. The band's giant riff-fests mark them out as the best UK heavy metal band never to have achieved greatness.

Diamond Head spearheaded the New Wave of British Heavy Metal of the late Seventies and early Eighties with Iron Maiden, Def Leppard and Saxon. Fuelled by Sean Harris's Robert Plant-flavoured voice and Brian Tatler's immense riffing, Diamond Head cut an independent EP, *Lightning To The Nations*—a cult classic—in 1980. A deal with MCA followed and in 1982 Diamond Head released *Borrowed Time*, featuring their undoubted masterpiece, the dark-hearted 'Am I Evil?'.

The nucleus of Harris and Tatler disposed of bassist Colin Kimberley and drummer Duncan Scott, bringing in Merv Goldsworthy (later of FM) and Robbie France for the recording of their misunderstood and maligned third album, *Canterbury* (1983). Overly ambitious at a time when Iron Maiden's back-to-basics traditionalism was topping charts, *Canterbury* was a heroic folly; Diamond Head crumbled. Burgeoning thrash giants Metallica and Megadeth each acknowledged their debt to Diamond Head—Metallica covered 'Am I Evil?' for their 'Garage Days Revisited' EP. As interest grew, Harris and Tatler reunited in 1992, and accepted a deal from the Bronze label. Megadeth's Dave Mustaine and Black Sabbath's Tony Iommi appear on the comeback LP.

DIO

Diminutive New Yorker Ronnie James Dio cut his teeth with the appropriately-named Elf, before founding Rainbow with former Deep Purple guitarist Ritchie Blackmore in 1975. (See also Black Sabbath in the Legends section, and Rain-bow below.) Over the course of four albums, Dio forged a reputation for a soaring, theatrical voice of a size inversely proportioned to his frame, and for a lyrical bent towards a Tolkienesque netherworld inhabited by ghouls, dragons, wolves and rainbows. On replacing bat-crunching madman Ozzy Osbourne in Black Sabbath in 1980, Dio cemented his status with the impressive *Heaven And Hell* and *Mob Rules* LPs before quitting the band after *Live Evil* in 1982.

Hitching up with weatherbeaten bassist Jimmy Bain, drummer Vinnie Appice and Irish guitarist Vivian Campbell, Dio bestowed his own name on the new band and created classic broadscape trad metal on the début release, *Holy Diver* 1983).

Holy Diver was a blueprint for Dio's entire career, and also its highpoint. Opening with the galloping 'Stand Up And Shout', and progressing through the romping title track and the parping pomp of 'Rainbow In The Dark', *Holy Diver* was both enormous and irrelevant.

Dio proceeded to repeat the formula with little regard for the law of diminishing returns. As the hyper-realism

Ronnie James Dio, whose soaring voice is in inverse proportion to his frame.

of thrash and speed metal contorted and redefined the boundaries of the genre, Dio's straight-laced traditionalism became increasingly incongruous. *The Last In Line* (1984) was a diluted *Holy Diver* and, when Campbell departed for lucrative tenures in Whitesnake and Def Leppard, the decline became terminal.

ENUFF Z'NUFF

Cheery pop rockers from Chicago, Enuff Z'nuff blend the spirit of Cheap Trick with tough guitars and Beatles-inspired vocal harmonies. Their self-titled début (1989) showcased Derek Frigo's incisive guitar and Donnie Vie's sparkling voice to better effect than two subsequent albums, *Strength* (1991) and *Animals With Human Intelligence* (1993), which allowed heavy-handed playing to outweigh some skillfully-wrought and thoughtful songs.

EUROPE

Euro-metal to the max and purveyors of dreaded melodic rock, Europe stood and fell by their major hit, that cheerfully silly parp through space, *The Final Countdown*.

Fronted by the squeaky-clean Joey Tempest, a heavy metal Osmond possessed of a thousand gleaming teeth, an enormous blonde bubble perm and the high registered vocal whine beloved of Scandinavian metal vocalists everywhere, Europe traded hits with Bon Jovi and Heart through pop metal's glory years, 1986 and 1987. Two domestic releases in Europe's native Sweden, *Europe* (1983) and *Wings Of Tomorrow* (1984) had preceded *The Final Countdown* LP (1986).

Building a vast teenage following on the back of *The Final Countdown*'s worldwide success, Europe pressed home their advantage with further hits. However, the band's pop appeal played against them. Unable to secure the strong heavy metal following established by Bon Jovi, Europe's next album, *Out Of This World*, floundered in the credibility gap. *Prisoners In Paradise* (1991) could not repair the damage.

EXODUS

Fundamental in establishing the influential Bay Area thrash metal scene of the mid Eighties, Exodus have never matched the bone crunching frenzy of their seminal début, the brutal *Bonded By Blood* (1985). 'Strike Of The Beast', 'A Lesson In Violence' and the title track evoked a precision, speed and violence surpassed only by Slayer. In 1985 Exodus appeared the equals of any of the West Coast soon-to-be giants, Metallica, Megadeth and Slayer.

Metallica poached the band's original guitarist, Kirk Hammett, to replace Dave Mustaine. Throat-shredding screamer Paul Baloff departed, to be replaced by Steve "Zetro" Sousa, and subsequent releases *Pleasures Of The Flesh* (1987), *Fabulous Disaster* (1989) and *Impact Is Imminent* (1990) lacked real substance.

EXTREME

From vague funk-metal beginnings, Extreme aspire to be the next Queen—all this on the back of one massive hit single, 'More Than Words', an acoustic guitar ballad!

Formed in Boston and floated on the back of heart-throb guitarist Nuno Bettencourt's studied pyrotechnics, Extreme's self-titled début (1989) disappeared without trace. A conceptual second set, *Extreme II: Pornograffitti* (1990), possessed a strong identity, although the band's funk work-outs appeared forced.

'More Than Words', a neat acoustic love song well sung by Gary Cherone, was a US and UK Number 1 hit.

Taking themselves extraordinarily seriously, Extreme produced a grandiose follow-up, *III Sides To Every Story* (1992), which included a tedious 40-minute orchestral piece, an identi-kit 'Hole-Hearted' in 'Tragic Comic' and more leaden funk in 'Rest In Peace'.

FAITH NO MORE

Faith No More are a band of extraordinary contradictions; a uniquely inventive and perceptive hard rock quintet, four-fifths of whom are scornful of the genre; a band who possess wit, grace and a searing power that is constantly threatened by petty internal wrangling.

Always eccentric, the nucleus of Faith No More—bassist Billy Gould, keyboard player Roddy Bottum and drummer Mike "Puffy" Bordin—came together in San Francisco, releasing a bizarre independent release, *We Care A Lot*, in 1984. The trio finally nailed down a steady line-up when they uncovered guitarist Jim Martin, a heavy metal man from the tips of his split ends to the points of his cowboy boots, and vocalist Chuck Mosley. Martin added stinging guitars to Faith No More's edgy, driving funk metal; *Introduce Yourself* (1987) was a patchy yet impressive major label début, fired up by the band's breakthrough hit, a new recording of the title cut from *We Care A Lot*.

Contrary as ever, Faith No More fired Mosley on the verge of major success. In came Mike Patton, a wet-behind-the-ears college kid.

With the metal-headed Martin firing scalding riffs over hard-driving tunes like 'From Out Of Nowhere', 'Epic' and 'Surprise! You're Dead', Patton's début, *The Real Thing* (1989) won instant critical and commercial acclaim, which was cemented with a heavy touring schedule and a live mini album, *Live At Brixton Academy* (1990). Patton, though, was reputedly ostracized by the band while touring, and he dallied with an utterly bizarre side-project, Mr Bungle, who released a self-titled album in 1991.

Faith No More enjoying a break between bitter fights within the band

For *Angel Dust* (1992), Martin added his heavy-weight riffs to tapes sent to him by the band, leading to accusations of his not pulling his weight. None the less, *Angel Dust* is Faith No More's finest album, by turns epic, spare, sarcastic and passionate.

A straight-laced but tongue-in-cheek cover of the Commodores' 'Easy' (for some reason retitled 'I'm Easy') provided a freak hit single to begin 1993, although privately the band were expressing doubts that they could continue to survive some bitter infighting.

Extreme (left to right): bassist Pat Badger, singer Gary Cherone and guitarist Nuno Bettencourt.

FOREIGNER

Foreigner, along with Journey, are the giants of their genre, the undisputed kings of AOR. Fronted by the honey-throated Lou Gramm, Foreigner broke ground with early hits 'Feels Like The First Time' and 'Cold As Ice' (both 1978), before cutting their epochal fourth album, *4* with producer Robert John "Mutt" Lange in 1981. *4* inhabits AOR nirvana. 'Urgent' is shot through with Junior Walker's funky sax break, 'Luanne' is exquisite pop metal, while in the great ballad 'Waiting For A Girl Like You', Foreigner cut a timeless paean to the glory of love.

Agent Provocateur (1985) was no disappointing follow-up. Gramm was still dogged by tragedy, as 'That Was Yesterday' and the monumentally melodramatic 'Down On Love' prove. Still not content, Gramm built himself up to fever pitch on guitarist Mick Jones's classic weepie 'I Want To Know What Love Is'.

Gramm and Jones fell foul of one another after the patchy *Inside Information* (1988), and Gramm enjoyed two solo successes, *Ready Or Not* (which just preceded *Inside Information* and *Long Hard Look* (1990) before forming the epic yet ill-fated Shadow King in 1991. Jones added Johnny Edwards—an unconvincing Gramm-o-like—for *Unusual Heat* in 1991.

The reunion all of AOR was waiting for, though, came in 1992, when Gramm and Jones buried their differences to cut three new tracks for inclusion on a compilation album, *The Very Best... And Beyond*.

FREE

Free split up in 1973, but their enduring influence prevails today in the music of bands as diverse as Foreigner and the Black Crowes.

Breaking out of the UK blues boom of the mid-Sixties and inspired by the godfather of the scene, Alexis Korner (who suggested their name), Free married loose 12-bar grooves with hard-hitting hooks. Paul Kossoff's spacious and sublime guitaring was a blissful foil for Paul Rodgers's soulful croon. Bassist Andy Fraser, barely 16 when the band formed in 1968, and drummer Simon Kirke laid a foundation both solid and fluid.

After two effortlessly classy albums in *Tons Of Sobs* and *Free* (both 1969), the band hit superstar status with the *Fire And Water* set (1970), which included the timeless 'All Right Now'– Kossoff's guitar break at the end of the track is surely one of the great rock solos.

The band split in 1971 after another hit single, 'My Brother Jake', but regrouped for more success with *Free At Last* (1972) and *Heartbreaker* (1973), Fraser having been replaced by Japanese bassist Tetsu.

Kossoff precipitated a final split by departing in 1973 to form Back Street Crawler. He succumbed to drug-related heart failure in 1976, on a flight to the US. He was 25. Rodgers and Kirke enjoyed continued acclaim in Bad Company.

Foreigner: juke box heroes.

GIRLSCHOOL

The raucous Girlschool were a band ahead of their time. All-girl metallic grunge now has its head with L7, Babes In Toyland and Lunachicks; Girlschool were caught in the tide of the New Wave of British Heavy Metal.

Guitarist/vocalist Kim McAuliffe and bassist Enid Williams were schoolmates. When they signed to the Bronze label in 1980 they had been augmented by guitarist Kelly Johnson, drummer Denise Dufort and bassist Gil Weston.

Forming an unlikely alliance with warty blasters Motorhead, they released a joint EP, 'The St Valentine's Day Massacre', in 1980, which enjoyed Top 20 singles chart action in the UK.

Demolition (1980) and *Hit And Run* (1981) were underrated LPs; the veteran Vic Maile's production lent a streetwise edge to some pleasingly basic bludgeon. Girlschool were stymied by conservative perceptions of "women in rock". Their Nineties revival, founded on a strong UK club following and a self-titled comeback LP (1992), proved them gutsy survivors. L7 *et al* owe Girlschool.

GUNS N' ROSES

See separate entry in the Legends section.

HANOI ROCKS

Fronted by the implausibly-cheekboned and girlishly beautiful Michael Monroe, Hanoi Rocks wore an aura of premature doom that lent glamour to their stylishly sleazy rock 'n' roll.

Formed in the unlikely glam stronghold of Finland (which also produced the excellent Smack), Rocks' members' names were their statements of intent; Nasty Suicide played guitar, Gyp Casino played drums, Sammy Yaffa looked great wearing his bass. Guitarist Andy McCoy, the band's major creative force, was inconspicuous by comparison.

After two domestic releases, *Bangkok Shocks, Saigon Shakes* (1980) and *Oriental Beat* (1981), the band relocated to London, replacing the unfortunate Casino with the lanky sticksman Razzle. In London, they became press darlings. Their next two releases, *Self Destruction Blues* (1982) and *Back To Mystery City* (1983), were fêted by rock critics; in retrospect the albums are studiously raunchy but ultimately lacking in genuine substance.

Two Steps From The Move (1984), was planned as a breakthrough release. It wasn't to be. Its failure was compounded by a disastrous US tour which came to a premature end when Razzle was killed while a passenger in a car driven by Motley Crue vocalist Vince Neil. Neil was convicted of causing the drummer's death, and was fined and sentenced to 30 days in jail. Neil got off more lightly than Hanoi Rocks. They disintegrated soon after

Razzle's death. Monroe cut an excellent solo album *Not Fakin' It* (1989) and then formed Jerusalem Slim with former Billy Idol guitarist Steve Stevens. The band split before the release of their début album.

HEART

Until 1985 and their watershed self-titled album, Heart's career boomed and busted like the US economy; since then, it's been on a solid, if unspectacular, course.

With a Led Zeppelin-inspired sound built around the partnership of the Wilson sisters—Ann, with a voice as spectacular as her frame, and Nancy, a cute and ballsy guitarist—Heart broke ground in their native Canada in 1976 with their début release, *Dreamboat Annie*,

which included the minor AOR classic 'Crazy On You'. A second album, *Little Queen* (1977), produced the enduring riff-fest 'Barracuda'.

Once established, Heart's form became patchy. *Private Audition* (1982) and *Passion Works* (1983) were as disappointing as *Dog And Butterfly* (1979) was promising.

A change of label, from Epic to Capitol, proved the band's salvation. Employing outside writers and sharpening their sound with studio techno-gloss, *Heart* (1985) produced two giant hits, the titanically-chorused 'What About Love' and the ethereal 'These Dreams'. The recipe proved easy to repeat. *Bad Animals* (1987) and *Brigade* (1990) enjoyed continued success.

Heart sisters Nancy (left) and Ann Wilson.

HELLOWEEN

The devastating first wave of thrash metal emanating from the West Coast of America in the early Eighties was echoed in miniature in Germany, traditionally a heavy metal stronghold. Helloween are among the best of German thrashers, but a spectacular beginning has turned sour in the face of an acrimonious and protracted contractual wrangle.

Michael Kiske's vocal wail was offset by the twin guitars of Michael Weikath and Kai Hansen. *Helloween* (1985) and *Walls Of Jericho* (1986) preceded the band's benchmark release, the conceptual thrash epic, *Keeper Of The Seven Keys Part I* (1987). This flamboyant fantasy provided the band with a strong

European base, which they exploited with the follow-up, *Keeper Of The Seven Keys Part II* (1988).

Poised for greater international success, Helloween ran into a brick wall. A switch of management to the powerful Sanctuary group—who masterminded Iron Maiden's stellar rise—precipitated a bitter split from their German independent label, Noise International, in favour of EMI.

A lengthy legal row prevented the band from releasing any product. Helloween recorded the bizarre *Pink Bubbles Go Ape* LP, which was available in the UK in 1991 before being withdrawn from sale in the ongoing dispute. Kai Hansen left to form Gamma Ray in 1991.

HELMET

Helmet are one of the first influential underground bands of the Nineties, blending indie cool with full-on riffage.

Led by Page Hamilton, formerly of Indie Darlings Band Of Susans, Helmet rose from the New York hardcore scene when they destroyed the PA at legendary venue CBGBs! A cool independent release, *Strap It On*, began a bidding war amongst major labels anxious to find "the next Nirvana".

A seven-figure deal with EastWest resulted in the brutal *Meantime* album (1992). Helmet are on the verge of crossover success.

Michael Kiske of Helloween, whose career hit a brick wall when the band moved from Indie label Noise to the giant EMI.

JIMI HENDRIX

The impact and ongoing influence of Jimi Hendrix's bewitching, revolutionary guitar playing is impossible to overstate; his echo can be heard throughout pop, rock, funk and blues as well as heavy metal. This elegant black man fused genres, he sucked in styles and threw them out again, translated into a heady, inspirational brew.

The current hysteria surrounding Seattle rarely mentions Hendrix, born there in 1942. After a stint in the US paratroops, Hendrix toured in house bands before British impresario Chas Chandler saw him play in Greenwich Village, New York.

Relocated to London and hooked up with bassist Noel Redding and drummer Mitch Mitchell in the Jimi Hendrix Experience, Hendrix took Britain by storm; the UK's finest players, Eric Clapton, Jeff Beck and Pete Townshend acknowledged a rare genius.

Hendrix was a showman, too. Handsome and dressed like a dandy, he embraced and then personified Sixties psychedelic style.

The Experience released *Are You Experienced?* in 1967. It was an artistic and commercial triumph. Hendrix had three successive Top 10 UK hits, 'Hey Joe', 'Purple Haze' and 'The Wind Cries Mary', a wistful lullaby reputedly cut as a B-side "live" in the studio!

Hendrix rarely put his guitar down; Chandler reported that he even took it to the toilet with him! In 1968, the Experience recorded two more albums, *Axis: Bold As Love* and the double set *Electric Ladyland*, Hendrix's acknowledged masterpiece.

Epochal performances at the Monterey festival and Woodstock inflamed his legend; Hendrix played with his teeth, set his guitar on fire, smashed his equipment. A shy and gentle man offstage, he gave every emotion full vent on it.

At Woodstock, he performed the US national anthem, 'Star Spangled Banner' as a mocking lament to Vietnam.

Hendrix's fame spiralled. He became a figurehead for rebellion, and his colour and politics told against him. As external pressures grew along with his intake of drugs, Hendrix split the Experience and formed Band Of Gypsies with drummer Buddy Miles and bassist Billy Cox. An eponymous LP was released in 1970.

Jimi Hendrix died a few days after playing the Isle of Wight Festival in 1970. Asleep after mixing drugs and alcohol, he choked on his own vomit. Live and retrospective releases now number in excess of 30, but you can hear Hendrix everywhere.

IRON MAIDEN

See separate entry in the Legends section.

†††

JANE'S ADDICTION

Jane's Addiction were a band of ambiguities. Formed in Los Angeles, they are far removed from the trashy rock 'n' rollers that Hollywood attracts; fiercely independent, they signed to a major label, but then refused to bow to commercialism; patently a band with a great deal to express, they split on the verge of crossover success.

Jane's Addiction's fulcrum was Perry Farrell, a bizarre, anarchic vocalist and lyricist, a gleeful subversive who effortlessly manipulated his image and who kept the band poised on a creative edge. Guitarist Dave Navarro, bassist Eric A. and drummer Stephen Perkins played ferociously for him, their dynamics allowing Jane's Addiction's music great breadth.

A self-titled, independently-recorded album on their own Triple X label generated intense interest; 'Trip Away', 'Pigs In Zen' and the beautiful 'Jane Says' were compelling evidence of Jane's Addiction's talents.

Their first release for Warner Bros, *Nothing's Shocking* (1988), proved Jane's Addiction were no flash in the pan. Free of financial constraints, their spacey and sonic power was given all its head on 'Mountain Song' and 'Ted, Just Admit It...'.

Now the hottest underground ticket around, and with Farrell provoking uproar with his refusal to bend to corporate will, *Ritual de lo Habitual* (1990) added commercial success to artistic acclaim. In the US, Farrell had the album released in a plain white sleeve with the Fifth Amendment to the US Constitution reproduced on it after stores refused to stock his papier mâché *ménage-à-trois* sculpture that adorned the cover.

Farrell split the band at their highest point, ensuring their reputation as the greatest underground act of the late Eighties remained intact. He took time out to set up the groundbreaking US Lollopalooza Festival tours before putting together a new band, Porno For Pyros, which includes Perkins.

JOURNEY

Journey are, of course, AOR's greatest exponents, creators of the classic American soft rock sound. Their impact on the genre and their greatest classic, their final LP *Raised On Radio* is expounded upon elsewhere in this book.

Founding guitarist Neal Schon conceived the band as a jazz-fusion outfit, but Journey's greatest moments came when his partnership with keyboardist Jon Cain and vocalist Steve Perry was established for *Escape* (1982). *Escape* encapsulated a direction Journey had been inching towards, sweetly melodic songs infused with warm guitars and Perry's majestic, often heart-rending croon. *Frontiers* (1983) was a worthy follow-up, and if *Raised On Radio* (1986) is, as it seems, Journey's last album, it is also their greatest.

Schon and Cain masterminded the release of an excellent retrospective box set, *Time 3*, which contains many rare and live recordings, in 1993.

JUDAS PRIEST

See separate entry in the Legends section.

KING'S X

Capable of both technological remoteness and great spirituality, King's X are a unique power trio sadly unable to convert huge critical recognition into large-scale appeal.

The band's epochal début, *Out Of The Silent Planet* was the result of a tight-knit sound honed on the grinding wheel of the US bar circuit. Some monstrous riffs ('Power Of Love', 'Visions') and sweet harmonics ('Goldilox', 'King') marked King's X out for greatness, but their three subsequent releases were stunted in the shadow of their giant début.

Gretchen Goes To Nebraska (1989) and *Faith, Hope, Love* (1990) became increasingly less direct and more convoluted. King's X's desire to be different ghettoized them as a minority appeal act.

Their self-titled fourth album released in 1992 recaptured some of their début's panache.

Kingdom Come, the Led Zeppelin soundalike act masterminded by former hairdresser Lenny Wolf (on the left).

KINGDOM COME

Fronted by a retired German hairdresser, Lenny Wolf, Kingdom Come caused a monumental furore with their self-titled début (1988).

Kingdom Come mercilessly plundered every major Led Zeppelin riff, and topped them up with Wolf's uncanny Robert Plant impersonation to create an album of such barefaced gall that one has to retain a measure of admiration for it! The album was a huge commercial success, with sales no doubt aided by Wolf's prickly and terse denials of plagiarism to the press.

A second album, cheekily titled *In Your Face* (1989), held back on the Zeppelin-isms and sales suffered as a result. *Hands Of Time*, a surprise third effort, retained the epic feel of the début without the more obvious reference points, and is the band's finest.

KISS

Kiss formed in New York in the early Seventies and created the ultimate rock image; bassist/vocalist Gene Simmons, guitarist/vocalist Paul Stanley, guitarist Ace Frehley and drummer Peter Criss were ready-made superheroes in their full face make-up and outlandish Buck Rogers chic.

Kiss's music—basic party metal—has long been derided by critics, but a whole generation of American rock bands, from Poison to Anthrax, Nirvana and Sonic Youth, were raised on Kiss.

The band's earliest work is their most celebrated and influential. The first album, simply titled *Kiss*, boasts five certified rock classics: 'Strutter', 'Cold Gin', 'Black Diamond', 'Deuce' and 'Firehouse'. *Kiss* is one of the great rock débuts, its songs as strong as the band's image, which in 1974 was primitive but was refined to cartoonish perfection by 1976 and the fifth album, *Destroyer*.

After the first three studio albums, Kiss cut a double live set, *Alive!*, at Detroit's Cobo Hall. *Alive!* sold so well that it kept the ailing Casablanca label afloat. After a further three studio LPs—including *Destroyer*, an epic Bob Ezrin production—came 'Alive II' and four solo albums, of which Paul Stanley's is a classic.

Kiss flirted with disco on their 1979 album *Dynasty*; 'I Was Made For Loving You', written by Stanley and pop metal hack Desmond Child, is a camp high-energy number sung in falsetto by tanley. The pop rock of *Unmasked* and confused conceptualism of 1981's *(Music From) The Elder* sapped the band's popularity, but they found salvation in a return to thunderous heavy metal. In 1982, Frehley left Kiss. In his stead came Vinnie Vincent, then Mark St John and Bruce Kulick.

Three years after *Unmasked*, Kiss finally dispensed with the greasepaint and became, sadly, just another ageing rock group. *Revenge* (1992) was a back-to-basics rocker, produced again by Ezrin, but it was no *Destroyer*. The long-waited *Alive III* was released in 1993.

KROKUS

An amusingly dumb Swiss metal combo, Krokus's unwavering devotion to brainless Euro-metal commands some grudging admiration. Led by the remarkable Maltese vocalist Marc Storace (formerly of Swiss rockers Teal), a man's man who sported an enormous bubble-perm and an unfeasibly hairy chest, Krokus's uninspired AC/DC-isms were enlivened only by the unintentional humour they contained; 'Long Stick Goes Boom', a clumsy sexual boast hysterically screeched by Storace, is a particular highpoint.

Other Krokus facts worthy of note are the band's early association with the Schmontz label and their first drummer, who plied his trade under the unfortunate name of Freddy Steady.

ss's god of thunder Gene Simmons unmasked and on stage.

LA GUNS

While lacking the inspirational fury of Guns N' Roses—the band LA Guns's tough guitarist Tracii Guns formed with W. Axl Rose—LA Guns earned a reputation for cool and sleazy rock 'n' roll in 5 years together.

After spluttering through multiple line-ups, Tracii Guns forged a strong partnership with former Girl singer Phil Lewis, a pretty Englishman best known for his well-publicized affair with actress Britt Ekland.

With the glamour of Hanoi Rocks and the gut-wrenching passion of Guns N' Roses largely absent, LA Guns none the less whipped up some convincing sleaze on their self-titled début (1987); tunes like 'Sex Action', 'Bitch Is Back' and 'Shoot For Thrills' say it all.

Cocked And Loaded (1989) refined the formula and featured a stylish slowie, 'The Ballad Of Jane'.

With a firm fan base established across the US and Europe, a third release, *Hollywood Vampires* (1991) emphasized the band's growing class, but was played out to a background of acrimony between Guns and Lewis. The pair split the band in 1992.

Guns put together the heavy-duty Killing Machine, while Lewis founded Filthy Lucre.

†††

LED ZEPPELIN

See separate entry in the Legends section.

LITTLE ANGELS

Little Angels's ordinariness seems no bar to success, at least in the UK. The founding quartet of Toby Jepson (vocals), Bruce Dickinson (guitar) Jimmy Dickinson (keyboards) and Mark Plunkett (bass) were just out of short trousers when they put the band together, hence the limp name they've since tried hard to play down.

Toby Jepson, frontman for pop metal stars Little Angels. The band were formed in the UK seaside town of Scarborough.

Little Angels have some grand notions about continuing the great British tradition of innovative rock bands, but the majority of their output is paint-by-numbers pop metal, neatly performed but hardly groundbreaking.

An independent EP, 'Too Posh To Mosh' (1987) led to a major deal with Polydor and instant success with their début LP, Don't Prey For Me. A boisterous set of Bon Jovi-alike tunes was coupled with the band's boyish grins for maximum teen appeal.

Young Gods (1992) repeated the dose, while Jam (1993)—a more mature set—entered the UK charts at Number 1 on the back of the mawkish acoustic single, 'Womankind'.

LYNYRD SKYNYRD

Lynyrd Skynyrd's guitar-heavy Southern boogie was a blueprint for the genre, and they supplied its greatest epic, 'Freebird', an initially wistful, ultimately fiery tune often imitated, never replicated.

When they were devastated by an aeroplane crash near Baton Rouge in 1977, which claimed the lives of rough-hewn vocalist Ronnie Van Zandt, guitarist Steve Gaines and his backing-singer sister Cassie, Skynyrd had cut seven albums of tough boogie; their first, Pronounced Leh-nerd Skin-nerd (1973), Second Helping (1974) and the posthumously-issued First And Last, proved particularly telling. (The band's impact is discussed at greater length in the Story of Metal section.)

A successful reunion, fronted by Van Zandt's brother Johnnie and initially marketed as a tribute tour, was effected in 1987.

The clamour for new product was met with Lynyrd Skynyrd 1991 and later The Last Rebel (1993), two sets that proved the spirit was still willing, even if the muse was often absent. Their live shows remain packed.

YNGWIE MALMSTEEN

No one possesses a higher regard for Yngwie Malmsteen's talents than the man himself. Ghettoized as a technically adroit guitar virtuoso, Malmsteen provides little in the way of songs to prove otherwise. He is the aspiring guitarists' guitarist.

The Swedish-born Malmsteen was "discovered" by Mike Varney, American owner of the Shrapnel label intent on building a stable of technically flashy young guitarists. Relocating to Los Angeles, Malmsteen joined Alcatrazz, a band fronted by former Rainbow singer Graham Bonnett. It was a move heavy with irony. Malmsteen's reputation as a clone of Rainbow's leader Ritchie Blackmore was hard won; he even wore the blouson and waistcoat outfits favoured by Blackmore.

Alcatrazz provided a base from which Malmsteen launched a solo career (his band, Rising Force, were, to all intents and purposes, a backing band only) which has been patchy in the extreme. Accessible, grandiose melodic rockers like *Odyssey* (1988, featuring vocals from another former Blackmore henchman, the hammy Joe Lynn Turner) and *Eclipse* (1991) were punctuated by almost unlistenable studies of technique like *Trilogy* and the quite dreadful *Live In Leningrad* (1989).

MANOWAR

Manowar are the ultimate heavy metal band, four broad-boned Vikings who cut open their chests in order to sign a record deal in their own blood!

With animal furs barely covering "Conan the Barbarian" physiques, Manowar laid down a sound to match; vast riffs, leather-lunged vocals, thundering drums, breakneck bass. Extremity is all. Manowar entered the *Guinness Book of Records* as the world's loudest band—official! In Joey DeMaio, they have the world's fastest bass player—listen to 'William's Tale' and then deny him! And no one holds a note longer or with more ferocity than Eric Adams.

In need of a narrator for the spoken passage in the gargantuan 'Dark Avenger' (from their 1982 début *Battle Hymns*), DeMaio approached Hollywood legend Orson Welles, who, amused by the cheek, agreed. His performance is classically hammy.

Battle Hymns's successor, *Into Glory Ride* (1983) re-emphasized the band's one-eyed vision, a vision so strong that it persists today, never stronger than in their 1992 set, *The Triumph Of Steel*, which includes the Cecil B. DeMille-scale 'Achilles: Agony And Ecstasy In Eight Parts'.

Manowar's intensity is best received in Europe and the UK—British fans' devotion was rewarded with the *Hail To England* album of 1984.

Manowar manfully accept the jibes that accompany grown men in loincloths, and never allow them to distort their unique approach.

MARILLION

At the forefront of the ill-fated progressive rock revival of 1982, Marillion advanced the tradition of classic UK progressive bands established by Genesis, Pink Floyd, Yes and ELP.

Fronted by the lofty, charismatic Scotsman Fish, Marillion's quirky Englishness quickly inspired a strong underground following after they'd established a steady line-up in 1981. Their early epics, the downbeat 'Chelsea Monday', a rasping anti-war diatribe, 'Forgotten Sons' and the medieval poem 'Grendel'—all lengthy, a wordy—left no one in doubt of the band's intent.

Marillion's début album, loquaciously-titled Script Fo A Jester's Tear (1983), entered the Top 20 in the UK Marillion exploded just as the other progressive band

Marillion in 1982 with singer Fish (centre).

following in their wake—Twelfth Night, Pallas, Pendragon—faded. Given the rapid dissolution of the scene that launched them, Marillion's continued success via a second release, the convoluted *Fugazi* (1984), was proof of their depth and commitment.

Eschewing fashionability, Marillion's watershed third album, *Misplaced Childhood* (1985) was a conceptual delve into Fish's psyche, 45 minutes of gentle melancholy that included a huge UK and European hit single, 'Kayleigh'.

Clutching At Straws (1987) was as bittersweet, and greater for its lesser introspection. 'White Russian', a spiky dispatch on the neo-facist rise in Western Europe, bit especially hard.

Fish quit the band acrimoniously in 1988 for a solo career. Marillion recruited Steve Hogarth and, based around Steve Rothery's aching guitar lines, matured into a rich hard rock band. *Seasons End* (1990) included a pastoral epic in 'Easter'; *Holidays In Eden* (1991) offered some winsome pop via 'No One Can' and 'Dry Land'.

MC5

Detriot's MC5 cut one of heavy metal's most influential obscurities, *Kick Out The Jams*, a ferocious live recording acknowledged as one of the first genuine metal albums. Rob Tyner's sonic wail characterized a bruising sound that made up in bludgeon what it lacked in finesse.

MEAT LOAF

Meat Loaf's 1978 album, *Bat Out Of Hell*, a titanic maelstrom of melodrama and excess, became the biggest-selling début LP of all time. Vast in every respect, it proved impossible to supersede, or even repeat.

Meat Loaf, a quivering 20 stones of blubber given to dressing in full evening wear at all times, sang *Bat Out Of Hell*'s overripe anthems of the agony of teenage love in a trembling baritone, but the vision encapsulated on the album was entirely that of Jim Steinman.

An eccentric New Yorker obssessed by William Blake, Gustaf Mahler and motorbikes, Steinman wrote all the songs and conceived the enormous, neo-classical sounds wonderfully evoked by Todd Rundgren's screaming guitars and magisterial, wide-screen, technicolour production.

Throat problems prevented Meat Loaf recording Steinman's planned follow-up, *Bad For Good* (which the writer recorded himself and released as a solo album), and so he returned with *Dead Ringer*—which touched *Bat Out Of Hell*'s heights on 'More Than You Deserve' and 'I'm Gonna Love Her Or Both Of Us'.

When Steinman split for success as a writer/producer, Meat Loaf floundered. No one can write like Steinman as a series of limp albums—*Midnight At The Lost And Found* (1983), *Bad Attitude* (1985) and *Live* (1987)—proved. *Bat Out Of Hell II: Back Into Hell* is, somewhat inevitably, now in production.

MEGADETH

Quitting Metallica is not a smart career move; it takes a character as fiery as Dave Mustaine's to succeed. Mustaine left Metallica in 1982 after personality clashes with Lars Ulrich and James Hetfield, and formed Megadeth in San Francisco with guitarist Chris Poland, drummer Gar Samuelson and four-stringer Dave Ellefson.

Their début, *Killing Is My Business...And Business Is Good*, was raw speed metal, all spitfire riffs and caustic lyrics. Boosted by some incendiary live shows, and Mustaine's outrageous, often dumb, public pronouncements, Megadeth bought a big cult following to Capitol for their major label début, and finest release, *Peace Sells...But Who's Buying?* (1986). The angry buzz of the title track was perfectly complemented by the barbed 'Wake Up Dead' and 'Black Friday'. The album has aged well. Its grind and flash still stand up.

Mustaine's uncompromising nature and loose lip damaged his public image. He disposed of Poland and Samuelson, bringing in Jeff Young and Chuck Behler for the recording of *So Far, So Good, So What!* (1988). It reproduced the speed and precision of *Peace Sells*, but lacked the spark, and marked the beginning of Mustaine's descent into heroin abuse. Turning his fighting nature to his own advantage, Mustaine cleaned up, and again reshuffled

Megadeth, recruiting hot young guitarist Marty Friedman and drummer Nick Menza. *Rust In Peace* (1990) was technically silky, punchy, full-on speed, with Mustaine relishing his newfound attitude. 'Hangar 18' was his finest song thus far.

Countdown To Extinction (1992) marks the maturing of Dave Mustaine. Still prickly, Mustaine has reined in his lip and let his intelligent, strong songwriting do the talking.

Megadeth leader Dave Mustaine, whose fiery nature led to his departure from Metallica in 1982.

METALLICA

See separate entry in the Legends section.

MINISTRY

Ministry's prime mover, the dreadlocked Al Jourgensen, is a godfather of industrial metal—a raging amalgam of electronic techno-beats, overdriven, grinding guitars and vocal samples.

Based at Chicago's Wax Trax studios, Jourgensen and partner Paul Barker inspire a burgeoning scene; Nine Inch Nails, Godflesh, Pigface and Murder Inc. are all blending sampling technology, harsh beats and some sinister imagery possessed of strong crossover potential. Die Krupps and My Life With The Thrill Kill Kult, giving fuller vent to dance and techno influences, are coming in from the other way.

Convincing independent releases led Ministry to a big deal with Sire and a rasping major label début, *Psalm 69. The Way To Succeed And The Way To Suck Eggs*. Led off by the abrasive 'Jesus Built My Hotrod', Ministry built a strong underground following.

It will only get more extreme.

MONTROSE

With hindsight, Montrose have grown in stature since their demise. Their blistering, self-titled début album (1973), forged on Ronnie Montrose's searing guitar playing, was an early demonstration of the depth of US hard rock. The future success of vocalist Sammy Hagar, now, of course, firmly established as a credible replacement for David Lee Roth in West Coast legends Van Halen, is a little ironic; Montrose had certainly pointed the way.

Paper Money (1974), was an inferior follow-up, and Hagar split for a solo career and a stint with HSAS before joining Van Halen.

Bob James sang on *Warner Bros Present* (1975) and *Jump On It* (1976), but the momentum was lost.

MOTHER LOVE BONE

Mother Love Bone was an essential and seminal influence on the Seattle scene, a bridge between the primitivism of Green River and the sophistication of Pearl Jam.

While Mark Arm's Mudhoney retained the garage spirit of Green River, Mother Love Bone refined rock roots and punk sensibilities into a vibrant, exciting sound.

The Green River axis of guitarists Stone Gossard and Bruce Fairweather and bassist Jeff Ament hooked up with drummer Greg Gilmore and flamboyant Malfunkshun vocalist Andrew Wood in Mother Love Bone.

A well-received independent EP, 'Shine', got the band a deal with Polydor, and a major label début with *Apple* (1990). A compelling blend of Gossard's Led Zeppelin fetishes and Wood's Bolan and Queen fixations, *Apple* provides some inspirational moments; the brooding 'Crown Of Thorns', 'Bone China', 'This Is Shangri-La' and 'Stardog Champion' are highpoints.

Sadly, Wood's predilection for Seventies excess extended to drugs. He died of a heroin overdose as recording was being completed.

Mother Love Bone were finished without him, but Gossard and Ament were not. They formed Pearl Jam with Eddie Vedder as they were cutting a tribute album to Wood, *Temple Of The Dog* (1991).

MOTLEY CRUE

Motley Crue's gleeful predilection for rock 'n' roll excess has contributed as much to their legend as their rumbustious and rudimentary glam metal.

Crue—blond bombshell Vince Neil (vocals), dark 'n' moody Nikki Sixx (bass), lean and handsome Tommy Lee (drums) and conspicuously ageing Mick Mars (guitar)—tottered from the LA club scene on stiletto heels, big hair teased up, lipstick and rouge as obvious as their high-energy, rapid-fire, bubblegum rock 'n' roll.

Crue were rude and gauche, and in Nikki Sixx they had not only a great-looking bass god but a shrewd mind which subtly redefined the band at every turn. The band

The classic Motley Crue line-up in 1991. From left to right: Mick Mars, Nikki Sixx, Vince Neil and Tommy Lee.

issued their début LP, *Too Fast For Love* (1981), on their own label, Leathur. It was a low-budget, low-life party album, loud, dumb and sexy.

Motley Crue signed to Elektra for their second release, *Shout At The Devil* (1983). The music—'Looks That Kill', 'Too Young To Fall In Love'—was more of the same, but the packaging was different. A pentagram on the sleeve and some well-placed hints at a satanic bent gave Crue a whiff of danger.

The band hit the UK for a a slot at the Donington Metalfest in the summer of 1984, and on their return to the US, disaster descended. Hanoi Rocks's drummer Razzle, a passenger in Vince Neil's car, was killed when the vehicle turned over with Neil at the wheel. Neil somehow escaped the incident with 30 days in jail, a large fine and a blight on his reputation which he has done little to acknowledge as yet.

Theatre Of Pain (1985) ditched the devil in favour of some fetching polka-dots. Recorded in the shadow of Neil's accident and impending sentence, the album was unconvincing. A cover of the bar-room rock 'n' roller 'Smokin' In The Boys Room' and a lumpy ballad, 'Home Sweet Home' just kept Crue on track.

When *Girls Girls Girls* emerged in 1987, Crue's dedication to rock 'n' roll excess took its toll. The album—more brash party anthems—broke big, and Crue's intake of sex, alcohol and drugs by their own admission had reached fever pitch. Their UK tour was cancelled

after the band ran riot in Japan. In December, Sixx collapsed of a heroin overdose and was declared clinically dead before his heart was restarted.

The incident precipitated a clean-up, and when *Dr Feelgood*—slick and saucy—was released in 1989, Crue celebrated their first US Number 1 album. A heavy touring programme cemented their fame and fortune.

After the band marked their tenth anniversary with the *Decade Of Decadence* compilation in 1991, they dispensed with Vince Neil as recording on a new LP began. Neil claimed that Crue were deserting their roots for a heavier musical direction. The Scream's John Corabi replaced him. Neil formed the Vince Neil Band with Billy Idol guitarist Steve Stevens, and they released their début album, *X-Posed*, in spring 1993.

MOTORHEAD

As British as fish and chips, Motorhead set standards in volume and severity that were only superseded by the emergence of Venom and thrash metal in 1981.

Motorhead's roots are in traditional rock 'n' roll; in their late Seventies heyday they played it tight but loose, "Fast" Eddie Clarke's souped-up, overdriven blues riffing was driven at breakneck pace by Phil "Philthy Animal" Taylor's machine gun drums and topped by Ian "Lemmy" Kilmister's heavyweight bass and throat-mangling growl.

Lemmy is a born rock 'n' roller, prominent warts and all. He came to London to roadie for Jimi Hendrix and

Motorhead's Ian "Lemmy" Kilmister—a born rock 'n' roller, prominent warts 'n' all.

soon found himself playing bass for psychedelic space-cadets Hawkwind. He named Motorhead after the last song he wrote for the band when he quit in 1975.

Original guitarist Larry Wallis and drummer Lucas Fox were ousted by Clarke and Taylor after one unreleased album (which eventually emerged as *On Parole* in 1980).

Lemmy's power trio gelled while cutting *Motorhead* (1977), but it was the *Bomber* album of the following year which marked the band's emergence. Raw and nasty and ear-threateningly loud, it was matched by the band's flat out live sets.

Overkill (1979) finished the job, a dirty affair that established the band as the UK's leading live metal attraction. When the landmark *Ace Of Spades* (1980) provided the band with their best material to date—'Love Me Like A Reptile', 'We Are The Road Crew' and the title track—Motorhead were primed for the recording of the epochal *No Sleep Til Hammersmith*.

Iron Fist (1982), was an underrated release, but Motorhead were being swept away by younger, more brutal bands. The ascent of thrash metal pushed back boundaries that only Motorhead had previously approached.

If the band's impact has diminished, their appetite has not. Lemmy remains the spine of Motorhead. Clarke quit in 1982, to be replaced by Thin Lizzy's talented but wayward Brian Robertson for the face-ripping *Another Perfect Day* (1983), and subsequently by Wurzel and Phil Campbell.

Motorhead made a belated—and unsuccessful—attempt at glory in the US when they signed to Epic for the *1916* album (1991). Lemmy, though, remains a benevolent, if prickly, godfather to a scene that would be a lesser one without him.

Mr Big

Mr Big began as a disparate cult "supergroup" of established hard rockers seeking a band identity, a challenge met with relish and burgeoning success.

Inspired by the classic British blues rock sound of Free and Bad Company, Mr Big are fronted by the big voiced Eric Martin, previously pursuing a critically acclaimed, commercially ignored career as an AOR cultist. Martin is backed by veteran bassist Billy Sheehan, formerly of Talas and David Lee Roth's backing band, dextrous guitarist Paul Gilbert, ex-Racer X, and drummer Pat Torpey, a well-travelled session man.

Mr Big was a persuasive début; individual talents were reigned in to ensure a cool hard rock groove best represented on 'Addicted To That Rush'.

Lean Into It (1991) included the breakthrough single, 'To Be With You', an acoustic ballad which topped US and UK singles charts. The less mainstream 'Green Tinted Sixties Mind' pointed to growing depth.

NAPALM DEATH

Napalm Death are the grand old men of the UK death/hardcore underground. The band broke through to an alternative audience after being championed by Indie guru and UK DJ John Peel, proving that hard grindcore music had a niche. Napalm Death deal in extremity; songs last anywhere from several minutes to one second, all are viciously played and inhumanly grunted.

Their 1987 début, *Scum*, made limited progress; *From Enslavement To Obliteration* (1988) broke through on the underground, and also on the US college circuit. *Harmony Corruption* (1992), a dull grind, proved the limitations of the extremes Napalm Death embrace; a fact borne out by each member's enthusiastic involvement in outside projects.

NELSON

Nelson are an astonishing sight. Blond twins Matthew and Gunnar Nelson—sons of the late country star Ricky—are male Barbie dolls; hair swinging about their waists, beautifully-sculpted faces just *impossible* to tell apart, tailored clothes not *quite* rock 'n' roll enough to upset anyone's grandmother.

The songs match the image. Their début LP, *After The Rain* (1990) is whiter-than-white AOR made for US radio. Lead-off track 'Love And Affection' is a quintessential American rock cut, glistening with guitars and imbued with sublime harmonies only brothers can provide.

NIRVANA

Nirvana's impact has been vast, their ascent rapid and seemingly unwanted by a band who retain the ethics of the garage scene that shaped them.

Nirvana formed in Aberdeen, Washington state, reportedly the archetypal dull logging town at the root of the gloomy Seattle grunge sound. Nirvana's attitudes are punk, their songs—for all their intensity—are blessed with glorious pop sensibilities.

Nirvana's garage days had their head on *Bleach*, a white-noise-fest of a début for Jonathan Poneman's Sub Pop label that was, none the less, an unreliable indicator of things to come. *Bleach*'s rudimentary grunge was, in the context of the oceans of it pouring from Seattle, strong, but hardly the stuff of greatness. In Kurt Cobain, though, Nirvana had a songwriter of great talent, and a sneering frontman to boot.

Nirvana raised eyebrows when they signed to David Geffen's hulking corporation, home to many of the fat cat rockers scorned and despised by Seattle's underground scene. *Nevermind*, though, brooked no argument. Propelled by 'Smells Like Teen Spirit', *Nevermind* rooted itself in the public consciousness with its rough hooks and Punk overtones. Rebellion and street cool was instantly available to anyone with the price of the album.

Cobain's brattish behaviour, and celebrity marriage to Hole's Courtney Love, thrust him into unwelcome limelight. A new compilation, *Incesticide* (1993) rounded up some loose ends, bringing together much bootlegged and rare material on one disc, and giving Nirvana breathing space to begin work on a new album reportedly heading back in the noisy direction of *Bleach*.

TED NUGENT

Mad, bad and the scourge of liberals, communists, anti-Americans and edible animals everywhere, Ted Nugent is a walking event, a huntin', guitar-playin', loud-mouthed *star*.

Born in 1949 in Detroit, Nugent was playing in bands before his schooldays were through. After gaining acclaim with the Amboy Dukes, Nugent found his star

Ted Nugent, the huntin', shootin', fast-talkin' motor city madman, currently starring for commercial rockers Damn Yankees.

on the wane as the band's career floundered. Never one to doubt his own ability, Nugent launched his solo career with a series of bizarre guitar duels against Frank Marino *et al*. Soon, the loin-clothed Nugent was the rock god he'd always considered himself. With his overdriven, fiery guitar spitting feedback and his onstage raps enhancing his wild songs, Nugent was on fire. *Ted Nugent* (1975), *Free For All* (1976), *Cat Scratch Fever* (1977) and the insane live album *Double Live Gonzo* marked his creative and commercial peak, although *Intensities In 10 Cities* (1981) backed up Nugent's boasts of his live prowess.

Nugent launched Damn Yankees with Styx's Tommy Shaw in 1990, and runs a parellel— and controversial—career as a bow-hunting guru.

OZZY OSBOURNE

While Ozzy Osbourne's greatest work was with Black Sabbath, his greatest success came with a solo career noted for its outrage and excess.

Ozzy was in despair on leaving Sabbath in 1979. He confesses to a lengthy drinking binge before pulling a new band together. Bassist Bob Daisley and drummer Lee Kerslake were journeymen, guitarist Randy Rhoads was anything but. His fizzing pyrotechnics inspired Ozzy; their writing partnership was a fine and productive one.

Blizzard Of Ozz (1980) was a lean and powerful set capped by the rollicking 'Crazy Train' and the Hammer Horror epic 'Mr Crowley'. America's youth clutched Oz to their bosom, parents looked on outraged. Ozzy's back-breaking tour schedule and another sizzling LP, *Diary Of A Madman* (1981) broke America.

Disaster struck when Rhoads was killed in a plane crash during Ozzy's 1982 US tour. In his sadness, Ozzy considered quitting for good. Instead, he bought in Bernie Torme and then Brad Gillis as temporary replacements—Gillis appears on a live LP of Sabbath covers, *Talk Of The Devil* (1982)—before settling on the dextrous Jake E. Lee for *Bark At The Moon* (1984). *Bark At The Moon* and its successor, *The Ultimate Sin* (1986), perpetuated Ozzy's legend without expanding his limited vocabulary.

Tribute (1987) was a live album recorded during Rhoads's brief but dazzling career. Jake E. Lee departed, to be replaced by Zakk Wylde, the least impressive

The madman Ozzy Osbourne. His greatest work was with Black Sabbath, but his greatest success was as a solo artist.

of Ozzy's partners. *No Rest For The Wicked* (1988) and *No More Tears* (1991) were workmanlike in the extreme.

Ozzy announced his retirement from touring in 1992, although his plans have been radically restructured by a reunion with Black Sabbath which took root at his final solo shows. Ozzy remains heavy metal's godfather, a warm and honest man who performs from the heart.

PANTERA

Pantera began 1993 as "the band most likely to succeed". Their brutal and raw power metal has—in the wake of Metallica's groundbreaking mainstream crossover—captured the imagination. Pantera, though, have taken longer than most to make their mark. They began by cutting three gaudy, Kiss-inspired glam rock albums.

Nearly all except the name has changed since then. Replacing vocalist Terry Lee with the youthful Phil Anselmo was the making of Pantera. Anselmo bristles with aggression; hair cropped short, muscular torso heavily tattooed, words drilled out, he is utterly convincing.

Cowboys From Hell (1990) redefined Pantera. Guitarist Diamond Darrell may be stuck with a dodgy glam name, but his savage riffing brooks little argument. The aptly titled *A Vulgar Display Of Power* (1992) sails close to Metallica, but Anselmo's uncompromising stance defies any real comparison.

PEARL JAM

Pearl Jam's monumental success—their début album, *Ten*, has sold 4 million copies in the US alone—has played against them on the ultra-hip Seattle underground scene. Their contemporaries, most notably Nirvana, have been scornful of their rich, sophisticated songs. Pearl Jam are unrepentant, and rightly so; *Ten* is an artistically pure release, and a classic début.

Guitarist Stone Gossard and bassist Jeff Ament pulled Pearl Jam together in extreme circumstances. Their previous band, the acclaimed Mother Love Bone, had disintegrated with the death of flamboyant singer Andrew Wood.

Eddie Vedder, a young itinerant, was down in California for the surf when he was given a tape of the new group. He immediately composed some lyrics and travelled to Seattle to join up. Gossard, Ament and Vedder were cutting *Temple Of The Dog*, a tribute album to Wood, at the same time as they began *Ten*.

Ten belies a grunge tag; it's no superficial garage racket. 'Black' and 'Oceans' are overlaid with piano, 'Alive' is a furious journey of self-discovery and 'Jeremy' a bleak sideways look at a disturbed and betrayed boy. Vedder's thoughtful lyrics, thick with conviction and conscience, and his soulful, roaring delivery are undoubtedly special. He has star quality.

†††

POISON

Poison can boast one of metal's fairytale starts: they rose from rags to riches with a début LP that cost just $23,000 to cut.

Look What The Cat Dragged In (1986) was a glam classic; instant, disposable trash bubblegum encapsulated by tunes like 'Cry Tough' and 'Talk Dirty To Me'. Poison had the looks to match. Singer Bret Michaels pouted forth from layers of cosmetics, guitarist C. C. DeVille

Poison guitarist C. C. DeVille, whose comic ineptitude led to his departure from the band in 1991.

stood proud beneath a mountain of blond candyfloss hair, bassist Bobby Dall strained against multi-coloured trousers, and drummer Rikki Rockett's name just about said it all.

Platinum first time out, Poison capitalized with ease. *Open Up And Say... Aah!*, their first LP following a major deal with Capitol, took advantage of a larger budget without losing the band's heart. A softly-strummed tearjerker, 'Every Rose Has Its Thorn', was a US Number 1 hit.

Poison slowly toned down the ultra-glam look, emerging as slightly tougher for *Flesh And Blood*, another mighty commercial hit, in 1990.

After such an untroubled rise to the top, Poison hit a major glitch as rock 'n' roll excesses took hold during a demanding touring schedule. The band crumbled when Dall slammed his hand in a car door and DeVille produced a comically inept performance at the televised MTV Awards in 1991. Both subsequently underwent treatment for drug and alcohol abuse. Dall survived in the band, DeVille departed for an as yet unproductive solo career.

Bret Michaels mixed a live album, *Swallow This Live* (1991), while he searched for a replacement for DeVille. He chose Richie Kotzen, a young musician who has enjoyed acclaim as a solo instrumentalist. *Native Tongue* (1993) was a strong, mature comeback.

QUEEN

Although Queen's massive pop success stands outside this book's remit, their early work—in particular their first four releases, *Queen* (1973), *Queen II* (1974), *Sheer Heart Attack* (1974), *A Night At The Opera* (1975), and their essential live album, *Live Killers* (1979)—was metal at its most persuasive, inventive, witty, overblown and powerful.

Fronted by the outrageously camp Freddie Mercury and fuelled by Brian May's relentless riffage, Queen produced some definitive metal—'March Of The Black Queen', 'Tie Your Mother Down', 'Brighton Rock', 'We Will Rock You', 'Death On Two Legs' and of course 'Bohemian Rhapsody' carved the band into legend.

QUEENSRYCHE

Queensryche are from Seattle but do not wear lumberjack shirts or hang around coffee bars, nor did they score bit parts in Cameron Crowe's *Singles* movie. Queensryche are from the old school; their first album *The Warning* predated the Seattle SubPop boom by half a decade, and took its cues from Judas Priest and Rush. Singer Geoff Tate has a shrill voice like that of Priest's Rob Halford, but has sported a quiff like Elvis's.

The quintet's second album *Rage For Order* combined complex classic heavy metal with an adventurous, FX-laden production by Neil Kernon, and around its release in 1986, the band misguidedly adopted a glam image. The third album was the watershed. *Operation: Mindcrime* was that most unfashionable of things, a concept album, but the music was powerful, original and anthemic, and the plot had everything; sex, death, drugs, suspense, religion, revolution and even a mysterious Dr X for a villain. Given its sharp political bent, *Operation: Mindcrime* proved astonishingly successful and thrust Queensryche into the platinum bracket.

Empire (1990) was a more straightforward and polished hard rock album with echoes of latterday Rush and Pink Floyd. The acoustic 'Silent Lucidity', inspired by guitarist Chris DeGarmo's experiments in lucid dreaming, was a massive US hit.

Queensryche have inherited from Rush the mantle of kings of techno-metal, and they wear it well.

QUIREBOYS

The Quireboys play a simple brand of rock 'n' roll weaned on the classic British rock groups of the Sixties and Seventies: the Faces, Humble Pie, Mott The Hoople and, principally, The Rolling Stones. Singer Spike, whose raspy voice recalls vintage Rod Stewart, has defined the pinnacle of rock 'n' roll music as the Stones' 'Tumbling Dice'. The Quireboys will never make an *Exile On Main Street*, but their live performaces are fun and the début album, saucily-titled *A Bit Of What You Fancy*, boasts a number of memorable songs; brassy rockers like '7 O'Clock' and 'There She Goes Again', and croaking heartbreakers like 'I Don't Love You Anymore'.

The quintet's second album *Bitter Sweet And Twisted* was many years in the making and something of a disappointment when it was eventually released in the spring of 1993 after much recording, rethinking and re-recording with big name producer Bob Rock (Metallica, the Cult, etc). Again, the Quireboys were packaged as a pop rock band, when Rod Stewart's epochal *Every Picture Tells A Story* is the kind of album they should emulate. The Quireboys are a good band who keep finishing runners-up to the Black Crowes.

Singer Spike of the Quireboys, "a good band who keep finishing runners-up to the Black Crowes".

RAINBOW

When sullen-faced guitarist Ritchie Blackmore quit the legendary Deep Purple, he formed Rainbow by poaching every member of Elf bar the guitarist! Elf's singer was the suitably diminuitive Ronnie James Dio, who later starred in Black Sabbath, then formed his own vehicle, Dio, before rejoining Sabbath.

Rainbow's début release, democratically-titled *Ritchie Blackmore's Rainbow*, was epic heavy rock. The LP sleeve portrayed a fantastic castle hewn from a giant Stratocaster—Blackmore's favoured axe. 'Man On The Silver Mountain' was typical of Blackmore's simple, majestic riffing and of Dio's myth-making. 'Temple Of The King' and 'Catch The Rainbow' also revealed a gentler side to the band.

Rainbow's second release was their masterpiece. The cover of *Rainbow Rising* depicted a huge fist rising from the depths of a raging sea to grasp a rainbow. The music was similarly heroic. 'Stargazer' is a colossus worthy of Led Zeppelin, Blackmore's mighty riff matching the scale of Dio's great storytelling. The opening 'Tarot Woman' is another titanic number.

Another studio album, *Long Live Rock And Roll*, and the unwieldy live double *On Stage* preceded Dio's departure and the acquisition of Graham Bonnet.

Dio was all hair and flares and "666" hand-signals. Bonnet slicked back his short hair and wore tacky shades as if he were some would-be Lothario fresh from a sin-

Superstar guitarist Ritchie Blackmore, who formed Rainbow after quitting Deep Purple.

gles bar. However, Bonnet's arrival inspired Rainbow's biggest commercial successes. *The Down To Earth* album spawned UK hit singles in 'All Night Long' and the unforgettable 'Since You Been Gone', and following the album's release in 1980, Rainbow made a headlining appearance at the UK's inaugural Castle Donington Monsters of Rock metalfest; Judas Priest, the Scorpions and Saxon ably supported.

Bonnet and journeyman drummer Cozy Powell—a veteran of Whitesnake, Black Sabbath, the Michael Schenker Group and, laughably, Emerson, Lake and *Powell*—were both replaced prior to the recording of Rainbow's sixth album *Difficult To Cure*. US singer Joe Lynn Turner gave the band greater transatlantic appeal, best exemplified by the jukebox standard 'I Surrender'.

Two unhappily poor albums ensued before Blackmore dissolved Rainbow to reanimate Deep Purple's definitive "Mark II" line-up.

RATT

Ratt were initially hyped as the next Aerosmith, but such adulation soon cooled after a series of weak albums, beginning with 1986's *Dancing Undercover*. Ratt were five Americans playing hard rock music, but in reality, that's all they had in common with Aerosmith. Ratt's cheesy pop metal had none of the depth or sheer style of Aerosmith's glorious, freewheeling rock 'n' roll.

Ratt's eponymous début EP was a boisterous affair featuring a cover of 'Walkin' The Dog', as popularized by Aerosmith. Their first full album, *Out Of The Cellar*, and its successor, *Invasion Of Your Privacy,* were loud, catchy, glitzy and made the band an overnight sensation in the US, but by 1986 the party was over. Ratt's formula had lost its magic. The group's sales dwindled until their demise in 1991. Stephen Pearcy formed Arcade with ex-Cinderella drummer Fred Coury.

RED HOT CHILI PEPPERS

The Red Hot Chili Peppers' American punk roots give their edgy funk metal an iron-hard base. The Chilis sound impressively abrasive, but their groove is too often overrun by aggressive playing. None the less, the band are a cool alternative to the US mainstream.

Vocalist Anthony Keidis and bassist Flea played together in punk outfit Anthem before Flea split to join LA hardcore legends Fear. The pair reunited in 1983 and were joined by guitarist Hillel Slovak and drummer Chad Smith. The Chilis signed to EMI and released their début album in 1984. Tough but stilted, it laid a firm foundation for *Freakey Styley*, a more rounded set produced by funk overlord George Clinton.

The Uplift Mofo Party Plan (1988) turned cult status into hard sales, led by heavy funk workouts like 'Behind The Sun' and 'Fight Like A Brave'. Slovak died from drug abuse in the summer of that year. The band brought in John Frusciante to cut *Mother's Milk*, their breakthrough 1989 release. *Blood Sugar Sex Magik*, the Chilis' first album for Warner Brothers, is their best work to date, capped by the massive US hit 'Under The Bridge', a winsome paean to their hometown of Los Angeles. Frusciante quit the band during their heavy 1992 touring programme. He was replaced by Arik Marshall.

DAN REED NETWORK

Reed is one of the finest songwriters of his generation, but has yet to score a major hit despite writing some brilliant pop songs. The Dan Reed Network is a multiracial group based in Portland, Oregon, and comprising a Hawaiian (Reed), a Japanese keyboard player, a black bassist and guitarist and a Jewish drummer. Reed was once told to ditch the black guys and a lucrative recording contract was his. The Network got a deal elsewhere.

Their first album is classic funk metal, described upon

its release as an amalgam of Prince and Bon Jovi. Some of the songs are pure funk (the lead-off track, 'World Has A Heart Too', is a taut funk chant lasting just a minute), some are pure rock ('Resurrect' is a thunderous rock anthem), but most of the songs are an effortless and natural, an uncontrived fusion of funky groove and rock guitar power. 'Tamin' The Wild Nights' is the big ballad but 'I'm So Sorry' is still more poignant, a powerful tale of teenage suicide.

Slam (1989) was more of the same; great uptempo tracks like 'Doin' The Love Thing' (hard funk with heavy metal guitar abuse) and 'I'm Lonely, Please Stay' (wonderfully simple pop), and beautiful love songs like 'Rainbow Child' (inspired by a girl Reed watched dancing barefoot and alone at a Grateful Dead show) and the languorous 'Stronger Than Steel'. Inexplicably, Reed shaved his head before the release of the third album *The Heat*, but the music did not alter radically. 'Mix It Up' is arguably Reed's most perceptive lyric, while 'The Salt Of Joy' is his epic, as Prince's is 'Purple Rain'.

By 1991 the Dan Reed Network had released three classic albums but had still not made the big commerical breakthrough predicted by many, but while Reed continues to write such brilliant songs, there is hope.

A shaven-headed Dan Reed before the 1991 release of the Network's third album, *The Heat*.

ROSE TATTOO

Led by bald singer Angry Anderson, a barrel of a man blue with back alley tattoos, Rose Tattoo were the hardest rock 'n' roll band in the world. Even their names—Angry, Mick Cocks, Geordie Leech—were hard. Raised on the Australian pub circuit, where machismo is all, the Tattoos had big muscles, big bellies, busted knuckles and faces like robbers' dogs. "Nice boys," yelled Angry, "don't play rock 'n' roll." Rose Tattoo played *hard* rock 'n' roll.

The début *Rock 'N' Roll Outlaws* was the Tattoos at their toughest and best. Guns N' Roses covered 'Nice Boys' on their 'Live Like A Suicide' EP. Rose Tattoo were meaner than AC/DC but lacked the Young brothers' genius for riffs. After two more albums, the original line-up had broken up and the band's music had weakened. Angry later starred in the third Mad Max movie, *Beyond Thunderdome*, and sang the love theme to Scott and Charlene's wedding in the Australian soap *Neighbours*.

DAVID LEE ROTH

Diamond Dave's solo career began even before he left Van Halen. Roth's first solo release was a mini-album, *Crazy From The Heat*, released in 1985 and featuring four cover tunes, including the Beach Boys' 'California Girls' and a typically ebullient medley of 'Just A Gigolo' and 'I Ain't Got Nobody'. Van Halen had fooled around with similar material on albums like *Diver Down*, which was half originals, half covers.

"Diamond" Dave Lee Roth. The former Van Halen frontman is metal's greatest showman.

Roth also planned a movie titled *Crazy From The Heat*, but Hollywood was soon forgotten as he assembled a group in the Van Halen mould, with former Zappa sidekick Steve Vai on guitar. Vai had rehearsed most of Edward Van Halen's tricks and threw in a few of his own. Roth's first full solo album *Eat 'Em And Smile* was an explosive set of brash hard rock, launched by the single 'Yankee Rose', an outrageous new US anthem promoted by an equally outrageous video. Roth's videos, conceived by and starring the Picasso brothers (Roth and manager Pete Angelus) are some of the greatest and funniest ever made.

The second album *Skyscraper* was slicker, and despite yielding a hit in 'Just Like Paradise', another of Roth's booming, sunny-side-up rockers, it fared poorly. Vai quit to join David Coverdale's Whitesnake and was replaced by neo-classical whizzkid Jason Becker, who under Roth's tutelage delivered a surprisingly earthy performance on the *A Little Ain't Enough* album, only to retire from the band through illness before the ensuing tour. That album also sold disappointingly, forcing Roth to rethink.

RUSH

Canadian power trio Rush began their recording career with a workmanlike heavy rock album, eponymously titled and inspired chiefly by Led Zeppelin, and remarkable only for Geddy Lee's shrill and somewhat goofy yelp. However, the departure of original drummer John Rutsey brought wholesale change in that his replacement Neil Peart was an imaginative lyricist who led Lee and guitarist Alex Lifeson off to the land of the concept album.

Throughout the Seventies, Rush records were dominated by epic tracks like 'By-Tor And The Snow Dog' and 'Xanadu', the latter based on Coleridge's 'Kubla Khan'. On 1976's *2112* and 1978's *Hemispheres*, whole sides of albums were swallowed up by single songs; sprawling, convoluted and loaded with metaphor and instrumental detail. *2112* also aroused controversy in the UK when the *New Musical Express* foolishly branded Rush neo-fascists after Peart revealed the album's inspiration to be Ayn Rand's individualist novel *Anthem*. Ironically, 'The Trees', a song from *Hemispheres*, celebrated the birth of trade unionism.

With a new decade came the first modern Rush album, *Permanent Waves*. Previously overwrought, Peart's lyrics grew simpler and stronger, and Rush even scored a major hit single in 'The Spirit Of Radio'. The band's music and Peart's words were strongest on 1982's *Signals*, on tracks like 'Subdivisions' (Peart's thoughts on suburbia set to an awesome techno-rock soundtrack) and 'The Analog Kid', on which Peart evokes the restlessness of youth. This song, and the beautiful 'Afterimage' from 1984's *Grace Under Pressure*, feature the best of Neil Peart's poetry.

Their most recent recordings have seen Rush strip down their music to its essence. The trio now recall the Police as much as Led Zeppelin. After 15 albums Rush fled the Mercury label and signed to Atlantic. On their 1991 album *Roll The Bones*, Rush sound as vital as ever.

JOE SATRIANI

San Francisco-based Joe Satriani has made just four albums but is already established as one of the greatest guitarists in rock history. Steve Vai, a peer and a former pupil of Satriani's, acquired fame and fortune gigging with big league rock acts David Lee Roth and Whitesnake. Satriani did it the hard way, making innovative and mostly instrumental music and finding notoriety principally by word of mouth.

Satriani's first two albums, *Not Of This Earth* and *Surfing With The Alien*, wowed fellow musicians, but his later work has a greater emotional depth. The *Flying In A Blue Dream* album boasts some of the most beautiful rock guitar playing ever recorded. Joe loves to show off just like any kid with his favourite toy, but he also understands that simplicity is genius. Such an understanding is evident in his 1992 work *The Extremist*, in the celebratory hard rock of 'Friends' and in the delicate textures of 'Cryin'. Satriani is the modern guitar genius with the popular touch.

SAXON

The "Barnsley Big Teasers", as they are affectionately known, emerged in the late Eighties as part of the New Wave of British Heavy Metal alongside Def Leppard and Iron Maiden. While Leppard and Maiden went on to sell millions of albums, Saxon did not, for two reasons. The Yorkshiremen had something of an image problem—to this day, singer Biff Byford is renowned as much for his unfeasibly bulging silver spandex trousers as for his wailing voice—and although they scored a couple of top 20 UK singles, Saxon's pounding heavy metal was always too stodgy to reap the big money in the US.

Nevertheless, Saxon cut some of the great British metal of the late Seventies and early Eighties. The quintet's second album *Wheels Of Steel* was their strongest, featuring three NWOBHM standards in '747 (Strangers In The Night)', the title track and the relentlessly heavy metal 'Motorcycle Man'. The *Denim And Leather* and *Strong Arm Of The Law* albums were equally solid, unpretentious and staunchly traditional, but in the mid-Eighties Saxon made a doomed attempt to conquer the US with a succession of hackneyed soft metal releases. Their cover of Christopher Cross's 'Ride Like The Wind' was particularly horrible and embarrassing.

Recent years have seen Saxon go back to the bread and butter of basic, loud heavy metal. And Biff can still work a crowd. "This one's about refugees," he whistled at a gig in 1991. "It's called 'Refugee'."

SCORPIONS

The biggest-selling German hard rock act of all time, the Scorpions have never been the most tasteful of bands. As if the title of their 1976 album *Virgin Killer* wasn't offensive enough, the cover pictured a naked pre-pubescent girl seen through shattered glass, the point of impact over her vagina. On a later release, *Animal Magnetism*, a dog sniffs at his master's groin.

Early recordings are definitive Euro-metal. The double live set *Tokyo Tapes*, mixed limp cock rock— 'Backstage Queen', 'Suspender Love'—with the pompous follies of Hendrix-fixated guitarist Ulrich Roth—'Polar Nights' *et al.* Roth, who replaced Michael Schenker, wayward younger brother of rhythm guitarist Rudolf, was in fact so obsessed with Hendrix that he wound up living with Hendrix's ex-lover Monika Danneman. When Roth was himself replaced by Matthias Jabs, the Scorpions developed a more polished transatlantic commercial hard rock sound. The *Blackout* and *Love At First Sting* albums gave the band a foothold on the US arena circuit, although their best work remains 1979's *Lovedrive*.

In 1991 the Scorpions scored a Number 1 single in virtually every European territory with a ballad, 'Wind Of Change', featuring a remarkable display of whistling by singer Klaus Meine!

Paul Quinn of Saxon, the "Barnsley Big Teasers", whose *Wheels of Steel* album is heavy metal at its most uproarious.

SEPULTURA

Sepultura's rise to international cult status is all the more remarkable given that the quartet emerged from a Third World nation with an underdeveloped music scene. Sepultura are still based in Brazil's second city São Paolo, and are by far the biggest heavy metal band South America has ever produced. They also play some of the most brutal thrash metal ever conceived, and the most precise.

Sepultura's first three albums were released by Brazilian independent label Cogumelo, the second and third being reissued by Roadrunner following the success of the fourth album and first worldwide release, *Beneath The Remains*. The latter is Sepultura's greatest work, dense, furious yet controlled thrash, heavily inspired by Metallica. The next album, *Arise*, was a little disappointing, lacking the sheer in-your-face impact of its forerunner, but Sepultura remain one of the premier underground metal bands of the Nineties.

Sepultura's name is a translation to Portuguese, the band's native tongue, of the Motorhead song 'Dancing On Your Grave'.

SEX PISTOLS

The Sex Pistols were surely the most infamous rock 'n' roll band of all time. Prime movers and exploiters of the punk boom of the late Seventies, the Pistols' capacity to shock the general public was matched only by the sheer power of their début album, a big inspiration to Nineties heavy metal icons like W. Axl Rose, Dave Mustaine and Sebastian Bach.

SKID ROW

Much of Skid Row's success can be attributed to singer Sebastian Bach, whose sharp cheekbones and beestung lips made him rock's pin-up boy of 1989, but who is essentially just a headbanging kid at heart and is arguably the most outrageous heavy metal frontman of his era, if not as enigmatic as W. Axl Rose. Aided by a couple of big tunes in 'Youth Gone Wild' and '18 And Life', Bach's personal charisma has carried an average metal band to platinum status.

Skid Row formed in 1987 and, after hustling Jon Bon Jovi for a couple of support gigs, were signed by Bon Jovi's manager Doc McGhee. The quintet soon had a recording contract with Atlantic via Bon Jovi's own label Jambco, and toured North America with Bon Jovi to phenomenal response. Skid Row's eponymous début album sold over a million copies in the US as the bozo rebel-

lion of 'Youth Gone Wild' and the hard luck story power-ballad '18 And Life' scored heavy rotation on MTV.

After the overnight success came controversy. Bach complained that Jon Bon Jovi and sidekick Richie Sambora were getting most of the royalties from Skid Row's album sales via the Jambco contract. The issue was later resolved, apparently after Sambora had paid Skid Row the money they felt they were owed

Skid Row's second album, *Slave To The Grind*, sold less than the début even though the band were special guests of Guns N' Roses on the biggest rock tour of 1991. *Slave To The Grind* was a much heavier work. With this belligerent street metal record, Skid Row proved they were more than mere pop metal starlets; the title cut and 'Get The Fuck Out' echo Slayer. Yet for all that, Skid Row could use another '18 And Life'.

SLAYER

Slayer's definitive work is *Reign In Blood*, still the heaviest metal album ever recorded. The Los Angeleans made two albums before this monster, and have cut another two since. Their first, *Show No Mercy*, was a routine thrash workout with plenty of cheesy satanic shock value, but 1985's *Hell Awaits* was a far more serious proposition. Suddenly Slayer's riffing had developed a simple power evocative of vintage Black Sabbath, yet delivered at several times the speed. The band's lyrics, too, had a new edge, a real menace.

tempo material like the title track and 'Mandatory Suicide'. The latter song was released as a single in a controversial sleeve picturing a young conscript who had hung himself in his bedroom upon receiving his draft letter. *South Of Heaven* itself reflected the amorality of the times; clearly, Slayer were growing.

Seasons In The Abyss (1990) is another incredibly powerful album and includes the macabre 'Dead Skin Mask', a song inspired by mass murderer Ed Gein, who wore the body parts of his mutilated victims, including their faces, which he expertly skinned from the skulls and preserved. This track and all Slayer's classic material features on the live album *Decade Of Aggression*.

LA thrash metal kings Slayer. From the left: Tom Arayo, Dave Lombardo, Kerry King and Jeff Hanneman.

Reign In Blood was nevertheless an unprecedented triumph. Producer Rick Rubin, who had signed the band to the innovative and celebrated Def American label which he founded with Russell Simmons, focused Slayer's music and stripped it to its very essence. Once mocked for their clumsy black metal imagery, Slayer were now the most terrifying band on the planet.

Rubin took Slayer to his new label Def American for the release of their fourth album, *South Of Heaven*. Having created the ultimate thrash metal record in *Reign In Blood*, Slayer wisely made no attempt to top it. On *South Of Heaven* Slayer slowed up a little, mixing breakneck thrashers like the anti-abortionist 'Silent Scream' and the simply breathtaking 'Ghosts Of War' with deliberate, mid-

SOUNDGARDEN

In 1991, Soundgarden emerged as a major new force in hard rock music with the bizarrely-titled *Badmotorfinger* album. The Seattle-based quartet have been dubbed "the new Black Sabbath", such is the strength of guitarist Kim Thayil's riffing and Chris Cornell's voice.

For all their full-on rock power, Soundgarden's music is invested with a wry sense of humour. *Badmotorfinger* is an obscure joke playing on the title of Montrose's classic number 'Bad Motor Scooter'. Soundgarden's début album was titled *Ultramega OK*, meaning, in the band's words, "that it's really not bad!" That album also features a song titled '665-667' in mockery of metal's obsession with satanic bad vibes.

Ultramega OK was a vibrant power-rock record cut for Indie label SST. It was followed by the band's major label début *Louder Than Love*, which was roundly panned by the UK rock press. Some of the criticisms have been revised following the success of *Badmotorfinger*, an album which has established Soundgarden as new masters of driving, riff-based heavy rock. *Badmotorfinger* marries the raw power of British metal pioneers Sabbath and Budgie to an intelligent alternative rock consciousness, creating new age heavy metal with a classic feel.

STATUS QUO

The Quo are not just a blue jeaned, headbanging legend of rock; they're an institution, as British as bacon and eggs. Quo mainstays Rick Parfitt and Francis Rossi formed the band in 1962 after a chance meeting at a Butlin's holiday camp in the English seaside resort of Minehead.

In their second decade, Status Quo cut some great rock tracks, notably 'Down Down', 'Whatever You Want', 'Wild Side Of Life' and 'Roll Over Lay Down'. Quo liked to keep things simple, and are renowned for their reliance upon just three chords. The band argue that several of their songs feature four or more chords. One such number, 'Marguerita Time', is a nostalgic waltz in the tradition of the great British knees-up; the band have peddled much of this kind of material for the latter half of their career, but after 30 years of top 20 hits and bums on seats, the Quo are immune to criticism.

STOOGES

Alongside the MC5, Iggy Pop's Stooges were one of the seminal late Sixties Detroit garage rock combos. Pop, née James Osterberg, fronted the band and was prone to bloody self-mutilation on stage. The Stooges' first album, eponymously-titled, featured the droning and much-covered 'I Wanna Be Your Dog'. *Fun House* (1970) was another ferocious, feedback-heavy rocker, as was the final Stooges album *Raw Power*, despite David Bowie's notoriously bad production. In the late Eighties, Pop returned to his heavy metal roots as a solo artist with the riffy *Instinct* album.

STRYPER

After black metal came white metal in the shape of coif-fured Los Angelean hard rockers Stryper, the most famous Christian heavy metal band, and the most ridiculous. The quartet launched their début album, *The Yellow And Black Attack*, in 1984, clad, of course, in waspish yellow and black stripes. Led by brothers Michael and Robert Sweet (guitarist/vocalist and drummer respectively), Stryper mixed pompous melodic hard rock with the most syrupy ballads imaginable. 'Honesty', from the *To Hell With The Devil* album, was especially twee, Robert Sweet's vocal reminiscent of *The Muppet Show*'s Kermit the frog! *To Hell With The Devil* itself was still more laughable and

Tim Gaines (left) and Oz Fox of hilarious bible-thumping pomp metal stars Stryper.

boasts the most hilariously overstated hard rock singing of all time.

Live, Stryper hurl bibles into the audience and deliver extraordinary anthems like 'In God We Trust' and 'Glory Glory Hallelujah' with a dash of Hollywood. Long may they spread the good word!

TESLA

Tesla are based in the California state capital, Sacramento, and are named after noted electrical scientist Nikola Tesla. The quintet's début album, *Mechanical Resonance*, is their strongest to date,

Jeff Keith (left) and Frank Hannon of American hard rockers Tesla.

featuring fine songwriting and a classically-styled hard rock sound in the vein of Montrose, AC/DC and Bad Company. The band see themselves very much as songwriters; bassist Brian Wheat has a well documented love of the Beatles, while Jeff Keith has a raw voice which owes more than a little to Rod Stewart. Tesla's second and third albums lacked the sparkle of the first, but a live acoustic recording, *Five Man Acoustical Jam*, proved just how good some of this band's songs are.

THIN LIZZY

Thin Lizzy were led by Phil Lynott, black Irish bassist/vocalist and self-styled ladies' man, and one of the greatest songwriters in hard rock history. Lynott was ultimately killed by the rock 'n' roll lifestyle, having created some of the finest rock records of the Seventies. Lynott also had a nose for, among other things, finding brilliant guitarists; Brian Robertson, Scott Gorham, Gary Moore, Eric Bell and John Sykes all starred for Lizzy over a dozen glorious years.

Bell's unmistakable guitar melody gave the band their first UK hit in 1972 with *Whiskey In The Jar*, but after the next LP flopped, Lynott replaced Bell with two guitarists to beef up the band's sound. There followed a run of six classic hard rock recordings, beginning with 1975's *Fighting*, ending with 1979's *Black Rose*, and including the watershed *Jailbreak* (featuring the signature hit 'The Boys Are Back In Town') and the in-concert double *Live And Dangerous*.

From 1980 until the group's demise in 1983, Lizzy's output was patchy, although Lynott was always good for two or three great songs per album; songs like 'The Holy War', 'Renegade', 'The Sun Goes Down', 'Hollywood' and 'Chinatown'. Lynott released two solo albums while a member of Thin Lizzy but his career never really took off once the band had broken up. The great man died from the complications of sustained drug use in January 1986.

Thin Lizzy's black Irish leader Phil Lynott, one of the greatest songwriters in hard rock history. He died in 1986.

THOR

Jon Mikl Thor was remarkable not for his music but for his feats of extraordinary physical strength. With his long blond mane and pump-muscled physique, Thor resembled the *Marvel* comics superhero of the same name and performed many dangerous stunts on stage.

Thor could bend iron bars between his teeth. He wouldn't even flinch as hammer blows smashed concrete blocks piled up on his chest. And best of all, he could blow up hot water bottles until they burst! His music, however, was rubbish.

THUNDER

Formed by three ex-members of failed London-based pop rockers Terraplane—guitarist Luke Morley, singer Danny Bowes and bald drummer Gary "Harry" James—Thunder shot to stardom playing basic, blues-based heavy rock in the tradition of British rock legends Led Zeppelin, Bad Company and the Who. Thunder's music is no match for that of their heroes, but their début album *Back Street Symphony* has some powerful cuts in 'She's So Fine', 'Until My Dying Day' and the rollicking title track.

TWISTED SISTER

New Yorkers Twisted Sister were built like dock hands and dressed like hookers. They played anthemic hard rock without subtlety, influenced primarily by Kiss and AC/DC. Frontman Dee Snider, a hybrid of Bette Midler and Hulk Hogan, was renowned for his confrontational approach to audience participation, and is fondly remembered for threatening a crowd of approximately 30,000 at the UK's Reading rock festival.

In the early Eighties Twisted Sister produced some boisterous rockers such as 'I Am (I'm Me)', but by the time the Atlantic label dropped the band in 1988, the songs were weak and the spirit gone.

After much procrastination with Desperado, Snider formed Widowmaker in 1992.

The five-man line-up for New York's Twisted Sister—they were built like dockhands and dressed like hookers.

UFO

After three lacklustre albums, UFO recruited teenage guitar progidy Michael Schenker from the Scorpions and rapidly developed into a brilliant melodic hard rock act. Schenker was a gifted player but an eccentric and unpredictable character whose departure in 1978, following various disappearances (one on the eve of a major US tour), sparked a series of line-up changes from which the band never really recovered. With Schenker, UFO created some classic rock on albums like *Phenomenon*, *Lights Out* and *Obsession*. Ironically, the band's masterpiece, the live double *Strangers In The Night*, was recorded after Schenker quit.

Ignominiously, the band dissolved in the late Eighties following a string of desperate albums, but was reformed in 1991 by founder members Phil Mogg (vocals) and Pete Way (bass). The comeback album, *High Stakes And Dangerous Men*, proved dull.

Subsequent to UFO, Schenker's vehicle was MSG, formerly the Michael Schenker Group and latterly the McAuley Schenker Group, following the acqusition of ex-Grand Prix singer Robin McAuley. MSG's unstable line-up included at one point former Rainbow vocalist Graham Bonnet, who was relieved of his position after drunkenly exposing himself during a disastrous pre-festival warm-up show. The best MSG album is the first, simply titled *MSG*.

STEVE VAI

One of the most brilliant rock guitarists of the modern era, Vai has recorded with Frank Zappa, David Lee Roth and Whitesnake, and has cut three solo albums. The first, *Flex-able*, was cheaply made and is the more esoteric. *Passion And Warfare* was issued while Vai was a high-profile and highly-paid member of Whitesnake, and features everything from blazing heavy metal pyrotechnics to subtle jazz-rock inflections.

VAN HALEN

See separate entry in the Legends section.

VENOM

Now a spent force making unremarkable records, Venom were, *circa* 1984, the most outrageous heavy metal band in the world. Cited as a major influence by Metallica, Venom formed as a trio in the north-east of England in the twilight of the NWOBHM, and released their début album *Welcome To Hell* in 1981. As its title suggests, *Welcome To Hell* is crude satanic black metal. The most

UFO's Pete Way and Paul "Tonka" Chapman in their Seventies heyday. The wayward British rockers recently reformed.

powerful of its songs is titled 'In League With Satan' and begins with a backwards message evocative of the possessed Linda Blair in *The Exorcist*. The music evoked Motorhead, only Venom were faster, heavier, nastier, and had only the vaguest mastery of their instruments.

Nevertheless, Venom created an epic 20-minute track, 'At War With Satan', in 1984, and followed it with the most over-the-top live show London's Hammersmith Odeon has ever staged, dubbed "The Seventh Date Of Hell". Venom made three great albums followed by a number of weaker releases and odd anthologies before the original unholy trinity of Cronos (bass, vocals), Mantas (guitar) and Abaddon (drums) broke up. The latter pair still trade on the Venom name, while Cronos is a fitness instructor.

WARRANT

LA cock rockers Warrant struck platinum with their début album *Dirty Rotten Filthy Stinking Rich*, only to be accused of hiring session players to handle all the difficult bits during the recording of the album. Warrant silenced the critics with a second major success in 1990's *Cherry Pie*, which featured more inane, sugary pop metal. For their third album *Dog Eat Dog*, Warrant forgot all about playing ballads in white tuxedos and simply rocked out. *Dog Eat Dog* was forgettable, *Cherry Pie* was not.

WARRIOR SOUL

Still a cult act, Warrior Soul have made three acclaimed albums of vibrant and highly political street rock. The quartet are based in New York and are led by Kory Clarke, one of life's ranters. Warrior Soul's thunderous music is anthemic yet atypical; they covered grim post-punk group Joy Division's 'Interzone' on their controversially-titled second album *Drugs, God And The New Republic*. At their fiercest, they are true prophets of doom. Their music is intensely committed and demanding.

W.A.S.P.

Led by lumbering guitarist/vocalist Blackie Lawless, Los Angeles-based W.A.S.P. virtually reinvented the term "shock rock". White Anglo-Saxon Protestants? Lawless claimed the band's name was an acronym of "We Are Sexual Perverts"! W.A.S.P.'s début single was titled 'Animal (I Fuck Like A Beast)', and was reissued by Music For Nations in a truly appalling cover featuring a dog straddling a woman.

W.A.S.P.'s first album, released in 1984, was sleazy hard rock, harder and dirtier than the likes of Motley Crue and Ratt, but the music was overshadowed by the

New York cult act Warrior Soul are true prophets of doom. Leader Kory Clarke is second from left.

controversy courted by the band. During W.A.S.P.'s live shows, Lawless drank blood from a skull, threw raw meat into the audience and drooled over a near-naked woman strapped to a torturer's rack. This was more than mere buffoonery. Lawless is no fool, and once the controversy had made W.A.S.P. infamous, he quit the shock tactics and went for the mainstream rock audience with slicker music.

Wildman guitarist Chris Holmes, vodka-swilling star of Penelope Spheeris's *The Metal Years* and a dead ringer for *Star Wars* monster Chewbacca, left W.A.S.P. in an acrimonious split in the late Eighties, leaving Lawless to indulge his rock opera fanatasies. Lawless is a big fan of the Who and W.A.S.P.'s 1992 album *The Crimson Idol* is Blackie's own little rocked-out *Tommy*.

WHITESNAKE

The biggest *double entendre* in rock, David Coverdale's Whitesnake were once adequately described as "a home for old bluesers". Incredibly, within a decade, former Deep Purple vocalist Coverdale had, after a farcical amount of hiring and firing, turned Whitesnake into a multi-platinum-selling arena metal act. Among the musicians taken into Coverdale's employ in Whitesnake were former Purple bandmates Jon Lord and Ian Paice, and a number of star guitarists including John Sykes (ex Thin Lizzy), Vivian Campbell (ex Dio; now with Def Leppard) and Steve Vai.

With hit albums like *Ready An' Willing* and *Come An' Get It*, Whitesnake achieved great success in the UK and headlined the Donington festival twice, but Coverdale longed to repeat the success in the US. *Slide It In*—a provocative title even by Coverdale's standards—took Whitesnake to the brink of US stardom before the *1987* album became one of the biggest-selling rock records of its decade; 8 million units were sold in America alone. With 'Still Of The Night', an epic rock track styled on Led Zeppelin's 'Black Dog', 'Here I Go Again' and 'Is This Love', Whitesnake were all over radio and MTV.

The next album, *Slip Of The Tongue*, was a comparative failure, despite Coverdale's protestations that Steve Vai had created "the finest tapestries since Hendrix's *Axis: Bold As Love*. Coverdale had in fact abandoned his and Whitesnake's blues-rock roots in pandering to the pop metal market. Coverdale disbanded Whitesnake following their second Donington headliner, and has since formed a somewhat unlikely supergroup with former Led Zeppelin guitarist Jimmy Page.

WOLFSBANE

Alongside the Cult and Diamond Head, Wolfsbane are among the UK's finest heavy metal bands. After making three albums they were dropped by the Def American label in 1991, but the Wolfies are not quitters; they recorded a live album, triumphantly-titled *Massive Noise Injection*, at London's Marquee club in early 1993.

Wolfsbane's massive noise is an amalgam of AC/DC, Van Halen and Motorhead. The best of their Def American work is the mini-album *All 'Hell's Breaking Loose Down At Little Kathy Wilson's Place*, including 'Steel', full-tilt metal as heavy as Metallica, 'Paint The Town Red', a feel-good rocker in the style of classic Van Halen, and an insane, sci-fi B-movie-inspired title track.

ZZ TOP

Extravagantly-bearded Texan power trio ZZ Top have, over two decades, cut some of the most powerful, soulful, groovy, witty and downright bizarre blues-based boogie-rock ever recorded. *ZZ Top's First Album* was released 1971 and features a simple, honest brand of blues and boogie. On 1972's *Rio Grande Mud* the trio began to develop fuller facial hair and their characteristic earthy, driving Tex-Mex border rock sound. 'Francine' and 'Just Got Paid' were the band's first surefire classic numbers.

Tres Hombres was their first classic album, opening with the pairing of 'Waiting For The Bus' and the throbbing mellow blues of 'Jesus Just Left Chicago', two songs which are still paired in ZZ's live set. Other highlights include the raw soul of 'Hot, Blue And Righteous', the lazy funk of 'Sheik' and the blistering 'La Grange', the band's tribute to the bordello which inspired the movie *The Best Little Whorehouse In Texas*.

Fandango (1974) was another blues-rock powerhouse. Half of the album was a live recording featuring stage favourites like 'Long Distance Boogie' (wherein guitarist Billy Gibbons recalls the day his paw told his maw, "You let that boy boogie-woogie!"). The second half included the saucy hit 'Tush' and the beautiful 'Blue Jean Blues'. To promote the next album, *Tejas*, ZZ Top shared stages with livestock—buffalo, rattlesnakes and buzzards—on their extraordinary "Taking Texas to the People" tour. The band then disappeared from the public eye for three years before cutting the *Deguello* album in 1979, for which the trio learnt to play brass instruments and billed themselves as The Lone Wolf Horns!

By 1980 and the release of *El Loco*, Gibbons and bassist Dusty Hill's beards had grown to legendary proportions. The punchline: drummer Frank Beard has no beard. On the cover of *El Loco*, the Top were pictured being apprehended in a desert smuggling dope, and a couple of the tracks on the album suggested that not all of the contraband had been successfully impounded. 'Heaven, Hell Or Houston' features a series of weird phone calls by Gibbons followed by a samba coda!

Eliminator was the album that made ZZ Top a household name worldwide. Tracks like 'Gimme All Your Lovin'' and 'Sharp Dressed Man' were as smooth and powerful as stretch limousines and the accompanying videos—all cars, girls and furry guitars—made the trio the most unlikely MTV heroes of the Eighties. On 'Afterburner' and 'Recycler' ZZ Top's music grew ever more mechanized, Beard seemingly redundant, but since signing for RCA the band have hinted at a return to basic blues rock.

Billy Gibbons (left) and Dusty Hill, two of the three blues 'n' boogie kings ZZ Top, taking Texas to the people.

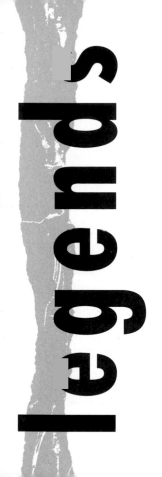

AC/DC

THE BAD BOYS OF BOOGIE

†††

Angus Young (guitar), Malcolm Young (guitar),
Brian Johnson (vocals), Cliff Williams (bass), Chris Slade (drums)
Formed: Australia, 1973

"IT LOOKED LIKE MURDERERS' ROW!" RECALLS AC/DC GUITARIST
ANGUS YOUNG OF ONE ESPECIALLY INTIMIDATING AUDIENCE THE
BAND ENCOUNTERED WHILE PAYING THEIR DUES IN THE PUBS OF THEIR
NATIVE AUSTRALIA, SURELY THE TOUGHEST GIG CIRCUIT ON THE PLANET.
"THE FRONT ROW WAS ALL BIKERS, AND THE LOOK ON THEIR FACES
WAS LIKE, SEND US THE LITTLE GUY IN THE SHORTS! SUDDENLY,
I JUST FELT A BOOT AND I WAS ON!"

AC/DC are one of the hardest rocking bands the world has seen. Had they
been any less, they'd not have made it out of those pubs, especially with little Angus dressed in his school uniform! Somebody suggested Angus wear
shorts, cap and tie to get the band noticed. It could also have got them killed,
but AC/DC were survivors; all of them, except singer Bon Scott.

Bon died in 1980 after a night on the tiles in London. He was left asleep
in a friend's car after a heavy bout of drinking, and with his neck twisted as
he slumped unconscious, Bon choked to death on vomit. It seemed incredible that booze had killed him. As Angus remembers, Bon was the guy who'd
drink till he fell over on stage, but he'd always get up again for the encore.

Not this time. February 20, 1980 was Bon's final curtain call.

At that point, AC/DC had just made the big league in the US following years of hard touring. *Highway To Hell* was the breakthrough album, the first of three bigsellers the band recorded with producer Robert John "Mutt" Lange. Before they hooked up with Lange, AC/DC were too bristly for US radio consumption.

Between 1974 and 1975, the band recorded two albums, *High Voltage* and *TNT*, for Australian label Albert before Atlantic culled the best tracks from each for AC/DC's worldwide début, also titled *High Voltage*. Like every AC/DC album since, *High Voltage* is a relentless boogie assault. A self-confessed "toilet wall graffitist", Bon spiced the band's simple, driving riffs with lyrics that were in turns filthy and streetwise. 'The Jack' is Antipodean slang for the pox, while 'Rock 'N' Roll Singer' and 'It's A Long Way To The Top (If You Wanna Rock 'N' Roll)' proved that Bon Scott was nobody's fool.

The next half dozen AC/DC albums are all classics, the strongest numbers from each also featuring on 1978's *If You Want Blood*, which the band recorded live on one night in Glasgow, their adopted hometown. *If You Want Blood* is one of the great live hard rock recordings. 'Whole Lotta Rosie', 'Problem Child', 'Rocker', 'High Voltage', 'Let There Be Rock'—it's just one killer riff after another.

On the album's cover, Angus's guitar is plunged into his stomach, blood staining his white school shirt and dribbling from the corners of his mouth. If this image was controversial, the next cover, *Highway To Hell*, was even more so. Angus wore horns and a tail and America's religious zealots were soon picketing their gigs. The closing track on *Highway To Hell* also stirred up trouble for the band, only this was more disturbing. The song, 'Night Prowler', is the most dubious AC/DC have recorded, but it was stupid rather than sinister. The band were shocked to find the song linked by newspapers to a spate of serial killings in the US. 'Night Prowler' is the sole blight on a brilliant rock 'n' roll album. *Highway To Hell* proved to be Bon's swansong, but it was more of a riot.

Led Zeppelin and Hanoi Rocks broke up following the death of a band member. AC/DC did not. Within four months of Bon's death, they found a new singer in Brian "Beano" Johnson, whose flat cap has become as much a trademark of AC/DC as Bon's tattoos and bare barrel-chest. Amazingly, Brian's voice is even more gritty than Bon's, and his lyrics just as dirty.

Back In Black was the first album AC/DC made with Brian. It is not only the strongest of their 15 albums, but also the biggest success, selling a colossal 10 million units in the US. *Back In Black* is a classic heavy metal album which its makers have struggled to equal with their ensuing six studio releases. Another live album was inevitable, and the band obliged in 1992.

And after 15 albums, they still haven't written a ballad! Now *that's* heavy metal!

AEROSMITH

AMERICA'S ROLLING STONES

†††

Steven Tyler (vocals), Joe Perry (guitar),
Brad Whitford (guitar), Tom Hamilton (bass), Joey Kramer (drums)
Formed: Boston, USA, 1970

WHEN ROCK WRITERS DUBBED AEROSMITH "AMERICA'S
ROLLING STONES", STEVEN TYLER WAS NOT HONOURED,
AS MOST ROCKERS WOULD BE, BUT ANGERED. TYLER, AEROSMITH'S
WIRY AND WIDE-MOUTHED FRONTMAN, FELT THAT SUCH
COMPARISONS WERE JUST A MEANS OF LABELLING HIM A SECOND
GENERATION MICK JAGGER. TYLER IS WRONG. AEROSMITH ARE
AMERICA'S ROLLING STONES BECAUSE THEY ARE AMONG THE
GREAT AMERICAN ROCK 'N' ROLL BANDS.

No Aerosmith record is as legendary as the Stones' *Exile On Main
Street* or *Sticky Fingers*, but Aerosmith are hugely influential. Guns
N' Roses, surely the biggest rock band of the Nineties, owe much
to Aerosmith, and even covered Aerosmith's 'Mama Kin' on
their début EP 'Live Like A Suicide'.

Where the Stones are driven by the Glimmer Twins, Jagger
and guitarist Keith Richards, Aerosmith had the Toxic Twins,
Tyler and guitarist Joe Perry, so-called due to the pair's noto-
rious hard drug intake. Both Toxic Twins have now cleaned

up. For Aerosmith and the Stones
alike, detoxification has brought
longevity. Both bands made much of
their greatest music while out of
their heads, but while a flow of hard
drugs was feeding their art, it was
also killing them. Aerosmith may
never make another *Toys In The Attic*,
but they are at least able to make
records in the Nineties.

The Bostonians' eponymous first
album was released in 1973. Tyler

Aerosmith's Toxic Twins Steven Tyler (left) and Joe
Perry.

cites the Yardbirds, the Beatles and James Brown as Aerosmith's key influences, and all are evident on the début. The piano led hit ballad 'Dream On' is Aerosmith's 'Let It Be', while the remaining seven tracks, all raw, full-blooded rock 'n' rollers, are pitched between The Yardbirds' blues-rock and "The Master" Brown's "super heavy funk".

On the second album, *Get Your Wings*, the band developed a heavier style perfected on the ensuing *Toys In The Attic*, which featured such classic rock tracks as 'Walk This Way', 'Sweet Emotion' and 'Toys In The Attic' itself. This and the following album *Rocks* represent Aerosmith at their decadent peak. Tracks from these two albums make up most of the epochal *Live Bootleg* recording.

Rocks was released in 1976 and stands alongside Van Halen and Montrose's débuts as one of the great American heavy rock albums. 'Back In The Saddle' is an outrageous opening number, its riff stumbling like a drunkard, Tyler's lyric characteristically innuendo-laden: "My snake is gonna rattle", etc. 'Rats In The Cellar' is superfast rock 'n' roll, while 'Last Child' boasts a strutting heavy funk riff and 'Combination' cruises like a Fifties lowrider. 'Nobody's Fault' is a slightly incongruous overtly political song, damning of America's interventionist foreign policy, but with 'Lick And A Promise' and 'Sick As A Dog' Aerosmith return to familiar themes before ending the album with a wailing love song, 'Home Tonight'.

The Seventies saw two more brilliant studio albums, *Draw The Line* and *Night In The Ruts*, the latter featuring the band's second recorded Yardbirds cover, 'Think About It', plus the killer one-two of 'Three Mile Smile' and 'Reefer Head Woman'. However, Perry quit soon after recording *Night In The Ruts*, his exit followed by the band's other guitarist Brad Whitford. One album was made in their absence: 1982's *Rock In A Hard Place*, on which Jimmy Crespo and Rick Dufay ably deputized. *Rock In A Hard Place* was a surprisingly strong release.

After a 3-year hiatus, Perry and Whitford returned as Aerosmith inked a new deal with Geffen. The first Geffen album, *Done With Mirrors*, was unspectacular and unsuccessful, described by one critic as "the work of burnt-out lugheads", but Aerosmith were not finished.

Permanent Vacation (1987) and *Pump* (1989) included songwriting by Desmond Child and Jim Vallance and resurrected the band's career with hit singles 'Angel', 'Dude (Looks Like A Lady)' and 'Love In An Elevator'. The hits were not the only songs of note: *Permanent Vacation* contained a spooky blues shuffle in 'Hangman Jury' and a swingin' pay religion satire in 'St John'; *Pump* housed the sinister 'Janie's Got A Gun', the bumping, mischievous 'F.I.N.E' ('Fucked-up, Insecure, Neurotic, Emotional') and the quaint, romantic 'What It Takes'.

The Nineties will see the 'Smiths return to the Columbia label, for whom they cut their first eight albums, in another lucrative deal.

BLACK SABBATH

THE HAND OF DOOM

†††

Ozzy Osbourne (vocals),
Tony Iommi (guitar), Geezer Butler (bass), Bill Ward (drums)
Formed: Birmingham, UK, 1968

BLACK SABBATH'S SOUND—ELEMENTAL, APOCALYPTIC AND BRUTALLY HEAVY—DEFINED HEAVY METAL IN ITS EARLY, CLASSIC FORM. HITTING ON A COD-HORROR IMAGE THAT ENTWINED PERFECTLY WITH THEIR CRUNCH-ING, DOOM-LADEN MUSIC, SABBATH CARVED A REPUTATION GREAT ENOUGH TO SURVIVE SOME TRAGI-COMIC LINE-UP CHANGES THAT BROUGHT JOURNEYMEN MUSOS, TWO FORMER DEEP PURPLE SINGERS AND A MALE MODEL INTO—AND USUALLY SWIFTLY OUT OF—THE BAND.

Formed in Birmingham in 1968, Sabbath's beginnings were ominously unpromis-ing. Rare Breed's hippy bassist Terry "Geezer" Butler replied to an advert placed in a music shop window by singer "Ozzy Zig", an unlikely moniker for an unlikely frontman—John "Ozzy" Osbourne, a reformed burglar.

Butler put Osbourne back in touch with schoolmate Tony Iommi, a gui-tarist who had lost the tops of two fingers on his right hand in a factory acci-dent, and who compensated by playing with the tops of washing-up liquid bottles on the mangled digits! Despite their mutual antipathy, Osbourne and Iommi stuck with Butler while he bought in drumer Bill Ward, and in 1970, the band—then titled Earth—cut an album in 8 hours of studio time and

renamed themselves after its title track, 'Black Sabbath'.

While Osbourne was just pleased to have something on vinyl to play to his mother, the album's raw attack, sinister undertones and goth-ic cover art ensured greater success. On completion of the album ses-sions, Black Sabbath travelled to Switzerland to complete a six-week residency in a strip club! They used the time to work up new material inspired by the primal soundscapes of 'NIB', 'Evil Woman' and 'The Wizard', tracks that were already gaining their début critical and com-mercial success.

Returning to the studio for a marathon-by-comparison eight days, Sabbath emerged with *Paranoid*, a set that perfected their low-tuned, monolithic black metal, and includ-ed 'War Pigs', 'Iron Man' and the ubiquitous 'Paranoid'.

The quartet cemented their rep-utation with *Master Of Reality*, cut and released in 1971, and some live shows of grinding brutality. By now, Iommi's endlessly inventive riffing, Butler and Ward's jazz-laden

Black Sabbath in 1990, with founder member Tony Iommi second from the right.

rhythms and Osbourne's mad wail had fused into an awesome unit.

Sublime and dark-hearted, Sabbath's 1972 release, *Vol 4*, remains their zenith. 'Wheels Of Confusion', 'Supernaut' and the turbulent epic 'Snowblind' capped two years of epochal creativity.

The first of many costly and labrinthine management wrangles delayed *Sabbath Bloody Sabbath* until late 1973, but the title track and the guargantuan 'Killing Yourself To Live' proved little had changed. With Sabbath's visceral live shows adding fuel to their rapidly escalating status, 1975's *Sabotage* was another highpoint, showcasing the rip-snorting 'Symptom Of The Universe' and 'Megalomania', a trippy epic. Mounting success bought mounting tensions within the band.

Osbourne and Iommi fought, while booze took its toll. The patchy *Technical Ecstasy* (1976) almost precipitated a split that finally came after the unfortunately titled *Never Say Die*, in 1979. Sabbath fired Osbourne, who embarked on a wildly successful solo career.

Osbourne's replacement, the diminutive and operatic New Yorker Ronnie James Dio, formerly of Rainbow, was an unlikely one, but doubts were quashed by the comeback LP, *Heaven And Hell* (1980). Song- rather than riff-oriented, *Heaven And Hell* kicked hard; 'Neon Knights', 'Children Of The Sea' and the title cut were outstanding.

After a solid follow-up, *Mob Rules*, recorded after Bill Ward left the band for personal reasons, Dio quit as a live album, *Live Evil*, was

being mixed. His replacement caused a sensation; Deep Purple screamer Ian Gillan was in for the lacklustre *Born Again* album (1983) and a farcical tour that culminated in the band building a "Stonehenge" stage-set that was too large to fit on a stage.

With Gillan—who later admitted his main motivation for joining was cash—out, Iommi cut a prospective solo album, *Seventh Star*, with another ex-Purple man, Glenn Hughes, on vocals. Record company pressure resulted in the album being released under the Sabbath name. Hughes, too, soon quit, along with Butler, and a discrediting and dizzying selection of workadays, including Ray Gillen, David Donato and Tony "The Cat" Martin joined Iommi.

Iommi and Butler reunited with Dio in 1992 for the limp *Dehumanizer* set, which was quickly overshadowed by a reformation of the original, classic line-up for a four-song jam in Costa Mesa, California, to mark the end of Ozzy Osbourne's rewarding solo touring career.

DEF LEPPARD

STEEL CITY SURVIVORS

†††

Joe Elliot (vocals), Phil Collen (guitar),
Vivian Campbell (guitar), Rick Savage (bass), Rick Allen (drums)
Formed: Sheffield, UK, 1977

SET AS A SOAP OPERA, DEF LEPPARD'S TALE WOULD BE
UNBELIEVABLE: A START IN THE UK STEEL TOWN OF SHEFFIELD, A DRUM-
MER WITH ONE ARM, A GUITARIST DEAD THROUGH ALCOHOL AND
DRUGS, FOUR-YEAR GAPS BETWEEN ALBUMS BESET WITH RECORDING
DIFFICULTIES AND UNFEASIBLE BUDGETS, AND YET REDEEMED BY BROTHER-
HOOD AND BARNSTORMING SUCCESS.

Along with their "sixth member", producer Mutt Lange, Def Leppard have
honed their brash, exuberant hard rock into the peak of studio perfection.
Their landmark releases, *Pyromania* and *Hysteria*, are as hard and unflawed as
glass; engineered nirvana.

In 1977, fledgling guitarists Rick Savage and Pete Willis were holding down
menial jobs and cranking out hard rock standards in rehearsals for a then non-
existent band. Joe Elliott, an 18-year-old van driver, tried out for the vacant
drum stool but turned to vocals in the absence of suitable candidates. Steve
Clark, an introverted lathe operator who'd been playing guitar since the age
of 10, soon relegated Savage to bass. With a line-up completed by drummer
Tony Kenning, the band adopted their bizarre moniker from an imaginary
concert poster Elliott doodled on a schoolbook. Rehearsing in a vacant build-

ing, Leppard constructed a rough
set, and began gigging in pubs in and
around Sheffield.

By November 1978, the band
were playing five nights a week, a
big problem for their new drummer,
15-year-old Rick Allen, who spent
what little time in classes he did
attend catching up on his sleep.

Leppard borrowed a modest
amount of cash from friends and
family and issued an independent EP,
'Getcha Rocks Off', via their own
label, Bludgeon Riffola. They shift-
ed an astonishing 24,000 copies.

Def Leppard's début album, *On
Through The Night*, was cut and released in 1980 through Phonogram.
Produced by Judas Priest's desk-
driver Tom Allom, the LP does little more than showcase Leppard's
potential as songwriters.

On Through The Night gave
Leppard a solid following, which
they consolidated with 1981's *High
N' Dry*. Recording was delayed
while Leppard waited for Lange to
finish work on Foreigner's classic *4*
opus, but they used the break well
to refine their thumping ballad,

'Bringing On The Heart-break', and the high-spirited 'Let It Go'.

Pete Willis was sacked in 1982, with the follow-up to *High N' Dry* well behind schedule and the guitarist battling with the bottle. Leppard replaced him with Phil Collen, formerly with glam titans Girl, who joined as the backing tracks for a new LP, *Pyromania,* were being completed.

Released in 1983, and led off by the infectious hit single 'Photograph', *Pyromania* dominated US charts for a year.

Def Leppard's success was soon to be undermined though, as *Pyromania's* follow-up looked doomed. A disastrous dalliance with producer Jim Steinman delayed things by an expensive year, and on New Year's Eve 1984, Rick Allen lost his left arm in a car crash.

His recuperation was long, and marked with awesome determination. Allen designed a revolutionary new kit that enabled him to trigger with his feet parts he would have played with his hand, and he made an emotional return to the band.

With Lange returning to hone *Hysteria* to a new high of technological perfection, the 1987 release, and year-long escalation in sales, completed Leppard's audacious recovery.

Hysteria shone, a bright catalogue of hits. 'Rocket', 'Women', 'Pour Some Sugar On Me', 'Gods of War' and the sublime title track heralded an avalanche of sales, over 12 million when everyone stopped counting. Leppard toured unstintingly, too.

Work on a new album was under way when Steve Clark, Leppard's doleful, wonderfully talented guitarist, overdosed on drink and pills at his London home. Elliott related a tragic story of an unhappy and insecure man unable to meet the pressures of stardom.

Once again, at their darkest, Leppard found undaunting spirit. They added to Clark's partially recorded parts to produce another hi-tech, hard-rockin' set, *Adrenalize*, in 1992. The road—with Clark's replacement Viv Campbell—seems to stretch ever on.

GUNS N' ROSES

APPETITE FOR DESTRUCTION

†††

W. Axl Rose (vocals), Slash (guitar),
Gilby Clarke (guitar), Duff McKagan (bass), Matt Sorum (drums)
Formed: Los Angeles, USA, 1985

GUNS N' ROSES FORMED IN THE MID-EIGHTIES IN LOS ANGELES AND OUTGREW THE LOCAL GLAM-FIXATED CLUB SCENE TO BECOME THE BIGGEST ROCK 'N' ROLL BAND OF THEIR GENERATION.

The five original members—W. Axl Rose (vocals), Slash (guitar), Izzy Stradlin' (guitar), Duff McKagan (bass) and Steven Adler (drums)—were each drawn to California from other states by Hollywood's enduring promise of fame and fortune. Axl and Izzy were friends from childhood in Indiana.

Guns N' Roses formed from the wreckage of two Los Angeles club acts, LA Guns and Hollywood Rose, and built a reputation for outrageous live shows. By the time the band has signed to Geffen after a furious record company bidding war, reports of Guns N' Roses's wild rock 'n' roll lifestyle made self-proclaimed "Bad Boys of Hollywood" Motley Crue seem like schoolkids smoking their first cigarettes. On their arrival in the UK for three shows at London's legendary Marquee club in the summer of 1987, the rock press dubbed Guns N' Roses "the most dangerous band in the world".

The hype was justified by the début album *Appetite For Destruction*. Guns N' Roses's first recording, a locally-released EP 'Live Like A Suicide', was tough, convincing, Aerosmith-influenced street rock, but *Appetite For Destruction* combined the band's furious punk energy with great songwriting. The watershed single 'Sweet Child O' Mine' showed a tender side to Guns N' Roses, its lyrics uncharacteriscally vulnerable amid all the talk of violence ('It's So Easy'), sex ('Rocket Queen'), alchohol ('Nightrain') and drugs ('Mr Bownstone', 'My Michelle').

Like the Sex Pistols, Guns N' Roses made rock 'n' roll shocking and exciting again. Their next release, in 1988, was a stop-gap mini-album *GN'R Lies*, featuring four new songs plus the whole of 'Live Like A Suicide', reissued by popular demand. In one of the new songs, 'One In A Million', Axl ranted foolishly: "Immigrants and faggots, they make no sense to me, they come to our country and spread some fucking disease." The singer later revealed that his homophobia is rooted in his childhood, alleging that as an infant he was sex-

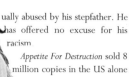

ually abused by his stepfather. He has offered no excuse for his racism.

Appetite For Destruction sold 8 million copies in the US alone as the band toured for 18 months after its release. Most people in LA thought Guns N' Roses would be lucky to last a week on the road! They nearly split in 1989 when Axl tired of other members' drug habits and announced that the shows Guns N' Roses were playing as support to the Rolling Stones would be their last, but somehow they held it together. There have been casualties; Adler was fired and replaced by former Cult drummer Matt Sorum, and soon after the release of the *Use Your Illusion* albums in 1991, Stradlin quit and was replaced by Gilby Clarke.

Only Guns N' Roses would release their second and third albums simultaneously! The band had too much material even for a double album, so two full-length albums—*Use Your Illusion I* and *II*—were issued in the summer of 1991. Inevitably, some of the 30 songs are weak, notably the impetuous 'Back Off Bitch' and 'Get In The Ring', and the covers of Wings' 'Live And Let Die' and Bob Dylan's 'Knockin' On Heaven's Door'. However, 'Double Talkin' Jive' is as mean as anything Guns N' Roses have recorded, 'Civil War' is a genuine rock classic and 'Estranged' is the finest song Axl Rose has written.

The subsequent tour brought with it new controversies. The band frequently kept fans waiting for hours on end before going on stage, apparently at Rose's whim. A gig in St Louis, Missouri, ended abruptly after Rose dived into the crowd and attacked a fan who was attempting to photograph the band. Rose was later charged with assault.

Guns N' Roses are still the most controversial rock 'n' roll band in the world, and Axl Rose, for all his sins, is the rock star of the Nineties.

Guns N' Roses's controversial frontman W. Axl Rose live on stage.

IRON MAIDEN

WARRIORS OF GENGHIS KHAN

†††

Steve Harris (bass), Bruce Dickinson (vocals),
Dave Murray (guitar), Jannick Gers (guitar), Nicko McBrain (drums)
Formed: London, UK, 1976

FORMED IN LONDON'S EAST END IN 1976—
WORKING-CLASS BOYS MADE GOOD—IRON MAIDEN ARE MORE
PROOF THAT AGGRESSIVE MUSIC IS MADE BEST BY PEOPLE WITH A
GENUINE BELIEF IN IT AS A MEANS OF ESCAPING A MUNDANE EXISTENCE,
A THEORY BORNE OUT BY BOTH METAL AND RAP.

From modest beginnings, Iron Maiden took their trad metal—hard songs beset by mystical and mock-occult imagery—up to stadium size, accompanying it with enormous stage shows that have starred ever-larger versions of their lumbering skull-faced mascot, Eddie the 'Ead. As the quintet entered their thirties, their message became increasingly incongruous, but their popularity, especially amongst younger fans, remains undimmed.

Steve Harris, Maiden's hairy, tattooed leader and one-time apprentice professional footballer, first picked up a bass guitar at 17, a late start for a prospective four-string god. A stint with grizzled local pub band Smiler introduced the musically naive youngster to Wishbone Ash, early purveyors of the twin guitar sound Maiden would embrace.

Harris linked up with Dave Murray, a local guitarist. The pair ran through two singers before settling on Paul Di'Anno, a short-haired, leather clad, jack-the-lad with punkish vocal attack. A second guitarist, Dennis Stratton, and a drummer, Doug Samson, augmented the line-up for a lengthy string of gigs at an East London pub, the Ruskin Arms.

Iron Maiden cut a three-track demo in Cambridge in 1979, just as the NWOBHM—led by Barnsley's

Saxon and Sheffield's Def Leppard—was emerging amid fits of post-punk blues.

Maiden committed the three demo tracks, 'Iron Maiden', 'Prowler' and 'Invasion' to vinyl. Dubbed "The Soundhouse Tapes", the EP sold 5,000 copies and led to the band being offered a long term contract with EMI.

Replacing Samson with Clive Burr, Iron Maiden cut a single, a rasping rocker called 'Running Free', which earned the band a Top 30 chart position at the first attempt.

Iron Maiden, the band's eponymous first album, followed in April 1980. A raw collection of hot riffing, Harris's galloping bass-lines and Di'Anno's magnificently brattish vocals, matched by the first of many visceral Derek Riggs sleeves, the album was devoured by the band's already rabid live following.

A celebratory tour was interrupted by the departure of Dennis Stratton, to be replaced by former

Iron Maiden founder members Dave Murray (left) and Steve Harris.

Urchin guitarist Adrian Smith, Maiden cut *Killers*, a brutal set that remains their definitive release. Di'Anno's inherent aggression leant the band a streetwise edge that's long since blunted. An aural mugging, *Killers* is fiery and raw. 'Murders In The Rue Morgue', 'Purgatory', 'Drifter' and 'Killers' are unremitting and spare—classic British heavy metal.

The band toured hard in support of *Killers*, and the resulting tensions culminated in Di'Anno's departure; bassist Harris reputedly wanted to get rid of the punk edge. That was ensured by the choice of replacement, Bruce "Bruce" Dickinson. An ex-public schoolboy, Dickinson had fooled around with the uninspiring Samson, perfecting his warbling style. Harris recognized it as the sound Maiden sought to complete the transition to foot-down, traditional heavy metal.

Dickinson's first release with the band, 1982's *Number Of The Beast*, confirmed Harris's instincts. Led off by the hit single 'Run To The Hills', *Number Of The Beast* is a comic

fantasy run through with schlock-horror.

Astutely managed by bluff Yorkshireman Rod Smallwood, the band's ascent to stardom throughout the world was swift. Replacing Clive Burr with the larger-than life Nicko McBrain, Maiden refused to divert from type. *Piece Of Mind* (1983), *Powerslave* (1984), *Somewhere In Time* (1986) and the unwieldy concept set *Seventh Son Of A Seventh Son* (1988) bought endless variations on a successful theme. The band's epic live shows cemented their fortunes and their legend.

A massively attended headline show at the Donington Festival in 1988 remains their peak. Adrian Smith quit to form the limp ASAP in 1990, and his replacement, Jannick Gers, bought some overdue fire to *No Prayer For The Dying* (1990)—which featured a UK Number 1 single in the dumb anthem 'Bring Your Daughter...To The Slaughter'—and *Fear Of The Dark* (1992). Dickinson announced he was to quit the band for a solo career in 1993.

JUDAS PRIEST

THE METAL GODS

✝✝✝

Rob Halford (vocals), Glenn Tipton (guitar),
K. K. Downing (guitar), Ian Hill (bass)
Formed: Birmingham, UK, 1973

BATHED IN A METAPHORICAL HELLFIRE, LEATHER-CLAD, RAMPANT, CAMP AND FACE-REMOVINGLY HEAVY, JUDAS PRIEST ARE UNSTOPPABLE; COMIC AND MONSTROUS IN EQUAL MEASURE. DRIVEN BY BULLET-HEADED FRONTMAN ROB HALFORD'S UNBENDING DEVOTION TO HEAVY METAL, PRIEST HAVE NOT BEEN MELLOWED BY WEALTH AND SUCCESS; THEIR MOST RECENT SET, 1990'S *PAINKILLER*, IS THEIR MOST EXTREME.

Priest back up a catalogue of screeching, overdriven albums with a live show of tongue-in-cheek pomp and musical fury. Drums pound, twin guitars grind hellishly and Halford emits a wail that blasts like a foghorn and squeals like a stuck pig. Priest are simultaneously theatrical and uncompromisingly brutal—heavy metal embodied, awesome and hilarious.

An initial determination to escape the inevitable factory job that awaited the working-class youth of industrial Birmingham in the UK's depression of the early Seventies fuelled Priest's inception. Guitarist Kenny "K.K." Downing and stoic bassist Ian Hill recruited Halford after the singer harmonized to a Doris Day record playing on the radio in his house!

Augmenting the line-up with local guitarist Glenn Tipton and the traditional succession of drummers, Priest signed to the Gull label and cut *Rocka Rolla* in 1974. As the limp title suggests, *Rocka Rolla* was an uninspired collection which the band waited two years to improve on. They did, with *Sad Wings Of Destiny* (1976), a gothic and doom-laden album that included the seminal 'Victim Of Changes' and marked the beginnings of their classic, crunching sound.

Judas Priest quit the Gull label in 1977 and signed to CBS, a major label equipped to give the band financial clout. After settling on a permanent drummer, the uncharismatically-named Les Binks, Priest cut the *Sin After Sin* album, an LP that finally defined a direction that has not wavered since—raw and sonic songs accompanied by lyrics of a metaphysical bent, delivered by a singer in a perpetual state of over-excitement and usually cast in the role of prophet of doom. The outstanding track was 'The Sinner', a rollicking sci-fi epic peaking as Halford produces the imperious couplet "Fall To Your Knees/And repent if you please."

Halford now began to refine his look, adopting swathes of studded

action as Judas Priest rode in on the fledgling NWOBHM—Iron Maiden, Saxon and Def Leppard would, along with Priest and Motorhead, drag aggressive music out of the post-punk doldrums.

Having peaked in the UK, Priest's rampant attack finally broke down US resistance with 1982's *Screaming For Vengeance*. Priest neatly adopted new technology, incorporating blurring synthesizers into their harsh riffing. *Screaming For Vengeance* and the subsequent *Defenders Of The Faith* and *Turbo* were the aural equivalents of *Blade Runner*, given to atmospheric, often bleak, sci-fi.

Established as a top-drawing live band, Priest hammered home their success with 1988's *Ram It Down*, before releasing their most intense and extreme LP to date, *Painkiller*, in 1990.

Halford quit the band in late 1992, ostensibly to free himself from a record deal that prevented him from forming a power-metal solo project, Fight.

leather which even ran to a peaked cap and huge black bovver boots. He topped off the image by carrying a leather riding crop. Half metal god, half raunchy S&M freak, Halford bestrode stages like a camp colossus, inspirational and hilarious.

Priest cemented their reputation with a brace of releases in 1978, *Stained Class* and *Killing Machine*. *Unleashed In The East* was recorded, according to the sleeve, on the band's 1978 Japanese tour, although the running joke—that the LP should have been titled *Unleashed In The Studio*—referred to rumours of heavy overdubbing. No matter; *Unleashed In The East* is a classic heavy metal release, swaggering and hamming its way through electric versions of 'Exciter', 'The Sinner', 'Genocide' and the lyrically unsound 'The Ripper'.

The aptly titled *British Steel* (1980) was the watershed in terms of commercial success. The tunes were gritty and real, and Priest kept them succinct. It paid off. 'Living After Midnight', 'Breaking The Law' and 'United' all enjoyed singles chart

LED ZEPPELIN

HAMMER OF THE GODS

††††

Robert Plant (vocals), Jimmy Page (guitar),
John Paul Jones (bass/keyboards), John Bonham (drums)
Formed: London , UK, 1967
.Disbanded: 1980

LED ZEPPELIN ARE SURELY THE GREATEST HEAVY ROCK BAND OF THEM ALL. FORMED AMID THE LATE SIXTIES BRITISH BLUES BOOM BY EX-YARDBIRDS GUITARIST JIMMY PAGE, ZEPPELIN PLAYED ELECTRIC BLUES LIKE NO WHITE MEN HAD BEFORE AND FEW HAVE SINCE, WITH AWESOME POWER AND RAW SEXUAL ENERGY.

Page mixed traditional blues themes with prototypal heavy metal riffing. Robert Plant sang from the gut and the groin, a lad from England's north Midlands who appeared like a Norse god, all gold mane and swelling chest. John Bonham beat his drums with unparalleled savagery. And John Paul Jones played bass.

Legend has it that Led Zeppelin took their name from a joke by the Who's John Entwistle about a doomed supergroup that he and wildman drummer Keith Moon dreamt of forming with Page and Steve Winwood. Entwistle felt such a group would "go over like a lead balloon". Page heard the joke, liked the name, and ironically, during the Seventies Led Zeppelin became the biggest rock band on the planet. It is claimed that, over the last 20 years, Led Zeppelin records have outsold the combined totals of all the other artists on the Atlantic label. In America, Led Zeppelin broke all attendance records for rock concerts, some of which still stand, decades on.

Led Zeppelin's eponymous first album, released in 1969, was a spectacular début. It is the classic example of primal blues rock power. Zeppelin resurrected two of blues legend Willie Dixon's standards, 'You Shook Me' and 'I Can't Quit You Baby', and produced some strong original material. However, it was the quartet's second recording, simply titled *II*, which defined the Led Zeppelin sound.

The album's first track 'Whole Lotta Love' boasts one of the greatest and most distinctive riffs in rock history, while 'The Lemon Song' was pure sexuality, Plant imploring: "Squeeze my lemon...till the juice runs down my legs."

Led Zeppelin released both their second and third LPs in 1970. *III* is regarded as the most mellow of the band's eight original studio albums. It includes a couple of beautiful acoustic songs in 'Tangerine' and 'That's The Way', but also some deafening rock in 'Immigrant Song'

Led Zeppelin's guitarist, producer and magician (!), Jimmy Page.

("Valhalla, I am coming!") and 'Out On The Tiles'. The blues of 'Since I've Been Loving You' begins with Plant softly moaning and ends in shattering catharsis.

The group's fourth album, frequently referred to as *Four Symbols*, is their most celebrated. 'Rock And Roll' and 'Black Dog' are supreme heavy metal riffs, while 'Stairway To Heaven' is the ultimate rock epic. The closing track 'When The Levee Breaks', a blues lament driven by Bonzo's titanic drumming, is simply colossal.

Houses Of The Holy (1973) was patchy but yielded 'The Rain Song', one of Page and Plant's most elegant compositions. And in 1975 came the inevitable double album *Physical Graffiti*, a daunting body of work that had everything from the mighty, mystical 'Kashmir' to the throwaway 'Boogie With Stu'.

Led Zeppelin made two more studio albums—*Presence* and *In Through The Out Door*, both erratic—plus the indulgent live double *The Song Remains The Same* before John Bonham's hard drinking proved

fatal. The band split soon after Bonzo's death in 1980. A posthumous collection of outtakes, titled *Coda*, was released in 1982.

Led Zeppelin had seemed superhuman, the all-conquering Bacchanalian gods of rock. The death of John Bonham exploded the myth and condemned Page and Plant to fitful solo careers. Plant has recorded a string of slick solo albums and had a little fun singing old rock 'n' roll and swing with his occasional band, the Honeydrippers, who cut a mini-album in 1984. Page scored Charles Bronson's *Death Wish II*, then formed an unwieldy supergroup, the Firm, with former Free and Bad Company singer Paul Rodgers, which dissolved after two lacklustre albums.

A big-money Zeppelin reunion—with Son of Bonzo, Jason, on drums—has often been rumoured, but Page has now formed a new partnership with Plant imitator David Coverdale, ex of Deep Purple and Whitesnake. Plant, Page and Jones reunited on stage at the US Live Aid concert in 1985 to play an emotional 20-minute set.

METALLICA

METAL UP YOUR ASS!

†††

James Hetfield (vocals/guitar), Lars Ulrich (drums),
Kirk Hammett (guitar), Jason Newsted (bass)
Formed: Los Angeles, USA, 1981

LARS ULRICH WAS AN UNLIKELY MAN TO LAUNCH A HEAVY METAL
REVOLUTION. AN EXILED DANE LIVING IN SAN FRANCISO'S BAY AREA,
THE DRUMMER'S GRAND OBSESSION WITH THE RAUCOUS NWOBHM
OF THE EARLY EIGHTIES WOULD LEAD TO THE INCEPTION OF THE
PRE-EMINENT METAL BAND OF THE NINETIES.

Metallica's transition from spotty young speedfreaks to dark-hearted power-mongers encapsulates and then abandons thrash metal, and ends with a self-titled album that has driven state-of-the-art, extreme music towards mainstream acceptance.

From influences that took in the best of the NWOBHM—Diamond Head, Venom and Iron Maiden to the unlikely Welsh metalheads Budgie—Metallica produced brutally blurred soundscapes that have been refined, album by album, into carefully sculpted epics illuminated with grimly melodramatic storytelling.

Ulrich hooked up with James Hetfield, a driving rhythm guitar player possessed of a gravel-bedded voice that ranged from a convincingly sinister whisper to a rasping semi-shout, perfectly conditioned to the extremities of sound Metallica began to pursue.

Ulrich and Hetfield cut a track for the *Metal Massacre* compilation album, and then linked up with bassist Ron McGovney and guitarist Dave Mustaine. Mustaine was a fiery character, a flame-haired maverick whose aggression was not channelled solely into the rapid-fire riffing that set the band apart from the pack in Los Angeles clubland.

In the summer of 1982, Metallica gigged solidly in LA, and made their name when they stood in for Krokus when the crass Swiss metallers failed to show for a gig.

Ulrich was anxious to move back up America's West Coast to San Francisco, where the Bay Area was playing host to a hot club scene. Metallica's savage live intensity set them apart, but friction within the band grew. Mustaine departed, and he'd soon put together his own outfit, the frenetic speed metal breaknecks Megadeth. Ulrich and Hetfield also parted company with McGovney.

Metallica poached diminutive six-stringer Kirk Hammett from another burgeoning Bay Area act, Exodus, and former Trauma bassist Cliff Burton. Burton was a character, lank brown hair framing a laconic visage and legs permanently encased in bell-bottom trousers.

Metallica cut a stony demo, titled, in truely corny NWOBHM style, 'No Life Till Leather'. A deal soon followed, and the band relocated again, this time to New York.

In 1983, Metallica recorded and released *Kill 'Em All*, a naive and yet crunching début that was a mere appetizer for their 1984 release, the intense and brutal thrash metal classic, *Ride The Lightning*. Built on white-hot riffing and Hetfield's vocal ire, 'Fight Fire With Fire', 'Fade To Black', 'For Whom The Bell Tolls' and the blistering 'Creeping Death' were belligerent and awesome. *Ride The Lightning*—along with Exodus's *Bonded By Blood* and Slayer's hellish *Reign In Blood*—stands as a a definitive work.

The band followed *Ride The Lightning* with *Master Of Puppets* in 1986. Again, Metallica excelled in brutality; 'Battery', 'Welcome Home (Sanitarium)' and the lengthy title track were exercises in savagery. On the road in Europe with Anthrax, Metallica's success was placed in perspective when Burton was killed in a tour bus accident. The band regrouped when former Flotsam And Jetsam bassist Jason Newsted replaced Burton for a covers EP, 'Garage Days Revisited'. The band's fourth album, *...And Justice For All,* followed in 1988. However, *...And Justice For All* was marred by a lop-sided production that ensured Ulrich's drums were as loud as his personality. A 251-date tour confirmed Metallica's star status.

Superficially, Bon Jovi and Aerosmith knobsman Bob Rock were bizarre choices to tape 1991's *Metallica*, but with the band's sound stabilized and tamed to fit broadscape compositions like 'Sad But True', 'Wherever I May Roam', and the snappier 'Enter Sandman', the album became the year's biggest event, overshadowing Guns N' Roses's much anticipated *Use Your Illusion* brace in critical acclaim and sales. Metallica begin the new decade as heavy metal's premier force.

Metallica pictured with the late Cliff Burton (shown top left).

VAN HALEN

HOLLYWOOD PARTY KINGS

†††

Sammy Hagar (vocals), Edward Van Halen (guitar),
Alex Van Halen (drums), Michael Anthony (bass)
Formed: Los Angeles, USA, 1976

ORIGINALLY KNOWN AS MAMMOTH, VAN HALEN ROSE FROM THE LA SUBURB OF PASADENA TO BECOME AMERICA'S PARTY BAND OF THE EIGHTIES. IN SINGER DAVID LEE ROTH THEY HAD THE ULTIMATE PARTY HOST, THE CLASSIC SUN-BLOND CALIFORNIAN ROCK ADONIS AND ONE OF THE GREAT SHOWMEN OF HIS TIME. DIAMOND DAVE'S ONE-LINERS ARE LEGENDARY.

Roth could talk it up like Muhammad Ali pre-fight; yet Van Halen isn't just the David Lee Roth Show. The band have proved as much by continuing to fill US arenas with a new singer, Sammy Hagar, following Roth's shock departure in 1985. Nor was Roth Van Halen's sole superstar. The band of course takes its name from Dutch American brothers Alex and Edward Van Halen, drummer and guitarist respectively. Edward is one of the most influential guitar players in rock history who not only revolutionized heavy rock guitar, but took it to black dance and mainstream pop audiences via an outrageous solo on Michael Jackson's 'Beat It', from the biggest-selling album of all time, *Thriller*.

Van Halen's eponymous first album was issued in 1978 and has yet to be topped for guitar excess. Edward was the Hendrix of his generation, creating new sounds, new possibilities, and, like Hendrix, Edward was also a fine songwriter. *Van Halen* is full of glorious rock songs; 'Runnin' With The Devil', 'Ain't Talkin' 'Bout Love', 'Jamie's Cryin'' and 'Little Dreamer'.

Van Halen II set a precedent for the next four albums. The songs were great, but the delivery was irreverent, spontaneous, carefree. Van Halen sounded like they were just getting off on their own brilliance. They were the best and they knew it and loved it. *II* was recorded in just six days and is classic feel-good American hard rock, featuring the band's first Top 20 hit 'Dance The Night Away'. On 'Bottoms Up!' Roth and bassist Michael Anthony laugh as they harmonize, while on 'Beautiful Girls' Roth admits he's just "a bum in the sun"!

Women And Children First (1980) was a little darker and heavier, 'Fools' and 'Everybody Wants Some!!' featuring some extended jamming, 'Romeo Delight' one of Van Halen's most ebullient numbers. *Fair Warning* boasted some thunderous, strutting hard rock—'Mean Street', 'Unchained'—plus a weird aside in 'Sunday Afternoon In The Park'. *Diver Down* (1982) smacked of contractual obligation—half the songs were covers—but it's still a great record. There's high-energy rock—'Hang 'Em High', 'The Full Bug'—skiffle—'Big Bad Bill (Is Sweet William Now)'—and covers of Roy Orbison's '(Oh) Pretty Woman' and Martha Reeves's 'Dancing In The Street', and it's all overdone in style!

1984 spawned a worldwide hit single in the euphoric 'Jump', on which Edward traded his guitar for a synthesizer, but there was plenty of heavy rock action on the album, notably on the lewd 'Panama' and 'Hot For Teacher'. In 1985, a long-running feud ended with Roth being replaced by former Montrose vocalist Hagar, and the party was over.

Van Halen have recorded three albums with Hagar: *5150*, *OU812* and *For Unlawful Carnal Knowledge*. Each has sold well, but Van Halen miss Diamond Dave's sparkle. 'Dreams' was a strong successor to

Van Halen's legendary original frontman, David Lee Roth.

'Jump' and 'Top Of The World' is classic celebratory pop metal, but the band's music is now mostly workmanlike.

Roth's solo career began explosively with the *Eat 'Em And Smile* album, which co-starred another guitar prodigy, Steve Vai, and beat Van Halen at their own game. However, after the slicker *Skyscraper* album, Vai quit to join David Coverdale's Whitesnake, and Roth's fortunes waned. The great man's third solo record, *A Little Ain't Enough*, included some great tracks—'Hammerhead Shark' and the smoky 'Sensible Shoes'— but it sold poorly.

Without Van Halen, Roth has faltered, and without Roth, Van Halen are half the fun. Together, they made six of the greatest heavy metal albums ever released.

AC/DC

BACK IN BLACK
ATLANTIC, 1980

BACK IN BLACK

THE SLOW AND SOMBRE TOLLING OF A BELL BEGINS THE BIGGEST ALBUM OF AC/DC'S CAREER; NOT SIMPLY THE BIGGEST seller, but an unlikely triumph over tragedy.

During the intial stages of writing for *Back In Black,* AC/DC singer Bon Scott died following a night of typically heavy drinking. Until then, the band had seemed unstoppable, their most recent album *Highway To Hell* proving their most successful worldwide. Bon's death might have finished them, but didn't. They found a new singer in Brian "Beano" Johnson, a strangle-voiced, flat-capped man's man from the northeast of England, and they cut *Back In Black,* one of the great heavy metal records.

Despite the bell-ringing and plain black cover, *Back In Black* is not a mournful record. Bon celebrated life and AC/DC honoured his memory with ten tracks of classic hard rock, honed to perfection by producer Robert John "Mutt" Lange.

There's even a little black humour in a title like 'Have A Drink On Me'. Bon would surely have appreciated the irony. Typically, however, AC/DC's humour is of the locker-room variety. 'Give The Dog A Bone' is a stream of innuendo as ridiculous as anything cooked up by Bon, the self-confessed "toilet wall graffitist".

Each of the ten songs is a powerhouse. 'You Shook Me All Night Long' was the hit single but every song swings a mean hook. Little wonder that this, the band's most radio-friendly album, sold in excess of 10 million units in the US alone.

AEROSMITH

TOYS IN THE ATTIC
COLUMBIA, 1975

O NE OF THE SEMINAL AMERICAN ROCK RECORD-INGS, *TOYS IN THE ATTIC* SPENT MORE THAN 2 YEARS ON THE US Billboard chart following the success of the single 'Walk This Way'. A decade after its original release, 'Walk This Way' was a hit again when heavyweight rap duo Run DMC covered the tune with the help of Aerosmith vocalist Steven Tyler and guitarist Joe Perry. It says a lot

about Aerosmith that their own version of the song is infinitely cooler and funkier than Run DMC's.

Aerosmith have always drawn heavily on R&B, Tyler citing the group's principal influences as James Brown and the Beatles, while the world's rock press have dubbed them "America's Rolling Stones".

Toys In The Attic is the strongest and most complete of the Bostonians' 11 studio albums. 'Walk This Way' would stand out on any album, but there are many fine songs on *Toys In The Attic*, beginning with the hard and fast title track and ending with the fussy piano-led ballad 'You See Me Crying'.

'Uncle Salty' is sad and languorously beautiful, 'Big Ten Inch Record' mixes a swing feel with sledgehammer innuendo, and 'Sweet Emotion', one of this great band's greatest songs, builds from delicate "talking guitar" harmonics to a thunderous riff. It also contains one of Tyler's most amusing lyrics: "Some sweet talkin' mama with a face like a gent/Said my get up and go musta got up and went!"

BLACK SABBATH

VOL 4
NEMS, 1972

I N THE 2 YEARS 1970–2, BLACK SABBATH CUT FOUR SEMINAL ALBUMS OF MONOLITHIC RIFFING, ALL POSSESSED OF AN ELE-mental beauty that belied the four members' rough roots. Their ham-fisted stabs at schlock-horror lyricism—even the band's name came from a bill poster advertising a Boris Karloff B-movie—became stark backdrops for the raw and primal soundscapes fashioned by Tony Iommi's brutal guitar.

The band's eponymous début (1970) could boast the first horror-metal track, 'Black Sabbath', and some blues-driven riff-fests, ('Evil Woman', 'Behind The Wall Of Sleep'), *Paranoid* (1970) perfected dumb darkness ('War Pigs', 'Iron Man') and *Master Of Reality* (1971) coined a savage directness ('Children Of The Grave', 'Into The Void'), but it was *Vol 4* that had everything that

119

made Sabbath giants; groove, power, excess, madness, fun.

Vol 4 was recorded in Los Angeles—the band were already making money—and self-produced, though the inspiration behind 'Snowblind' and the bizarre 'FX' is hinted at on the sleeve-notes: "thanks to the great COKE-cola company of Los Angeles"!

'Wheels Of Confusion' opens *Vol 4* like a fist in the face, Iommi's power-riff meshing with Geezer Butler's turbulent bass and Bill Ward's wristy, jazzy percussion to form a wall on which Osbourne wails, his untrained voice fuelled by a big heart and leather lungs.

'Tomorrow's Dream' and 'Supernaut' are yet more examples of Iommi's constant inventiveness and the band's primal power, but ambition overcomes technique in the ballad 'Changes'. After the white-noise roar of 'Snowblind', 'Cornucopia', 'St Vitus' Dance' and 'Under The Sun' provide a gripping finale.

Vol 4 represents metal's most direct force at their creative, maniacal peak. Unmissable.

DEEP PURPLE

IN ROCK
HARVEST, 1970

IN ROCK JOINED *BLACK SABBATH, PARANOID, LED ZEPPELIN II* AND *LED ZEPPELIN III* AS THE CLASSIC RELEASES OF 1970, and marked out Purple, Zeppelin and Sabbath as the giant triumvirate who would define and shape the heavy metal genre.

Unlike Sabbath and Zeppelin though, Deep Purple did not immediately produce a telling formula. Formed under the decidedly uncharismatic moniker of Roundabout in 1967, the band dallied with an unconvincing, hippy-ish stance that produced one hit, *Hush,* in 1968.

Bassist Nick Simper and vocalist Rod Evans were to be Purple's Pete Bests, replaced by Roger Glover and Ian Gillan respectively. The pair joined temperamental guitar hero Ritchie Blackmore, large skinsman Ian Paice and extravagantly moustachioed keyboardist Jon Lord to complete the band's definitive 'Mark II' line-up.

With *In Rock,* Deep Purple blossomed. The album was sleek and epic in equal measure, driven by Blackmore's virtuoso guitar, Lord's overblown Hammond organ and Gillan's lung-defying screech.

'Speed King' was a sterling opener, and the hypnotic throb of 'Black Night' took the song to Number 2 in the UK singles chart.

'Strange Kind Of Woman' proved that Deep Purple could push back the barriers of straightahead rock 'n' roll songwriting, investing the track with a moody mid-section that showed Gillan had more to offer than his mighty bellow.

In Rock's highpoint, though, was the mesmeric 'Child In Time', a spacy, organ-based *tour de force* capped by a frenzied and sonic Blackmore solo and Ian Gillan's greatest vocal performance, howled and cooed in equal parts.

The Mark II line-up cut three more studio albums before their split precipitated a mind-numbing carousel of joinings and leavings.

DEF LEPPARD

HYSTERIA
BLUDGEON RIFFOLA, 1987

TWO MONTHS AFTER ITS RELEASE, *HYSTERIA* WAS BEING PRONOUNCED A FLOP. WHILE THE PRECEDING *PYROMANIA* HAD SOLD 6 million and elevated Def Leppard to superstar status, *Hysteria* was slow to repeat the success. The pessimist consensus was that Leppard had spent too long making the album—roughly 2 years from pre-production to final mixing—and had been forgotten by the UK and US publics in the process. Ultimately, after six major hit singles, *Hysteria* outsold *Pyromania*. It had to; *Hysteria* is the perfect pop metal record.

Producer Robert John "Mutt" Lange is Def Leppard's unofficial sixth member. Writing and arranging as well as producing, Lange has a flair for blending pop hooks with hard rock that made Leppard kings of American FM radio on both rock and Top 40 stations.

'Pour Some Sugar On Me' was the breakthrough US single, simple, even a little goofball, a massive chant built on a booming drum track. 'Animal' is a more sophisticated rocker, as hard and smooth as marble. 'Gods of War' is the sole heavyweight, epic number, while the album's title track is the strongest of three ballads.

As Def Leppard were beginning work on *Hysteria,* drummer Rick Allen lost his left arm in a car wreck near the band's home town, Sheffield. Amazingly, he recovered to play drums again with a customized kit.

GUNS N' ROSES

APPETITE FOR DESTRUCTION
GEFFEN, 1987

APPETITE FOR DESTRUCTION IS AN EPOCHAL ALBUM, FURIOUS, EXPLOSIVE AND GUT-WRENCHINGLY HONEST. AS IT SOLD IN ITS millions, and Guns N' Roses five Los Angeles street punks—boozed and brawled their way into the public consciousness via lurid tabloid headlines, cold-blooded reassessment of *Appetite For Destruction*'s impact became irrelevant and impossible. The album's success fuelled GN'R, whose gleeful embracing of the corny-but-fun sex-and-drugs-and-rock 'n' roll lifestyle in turn gave *Appetite For Destruction*'s hot-headed rock anthems new significance.

Guns N' Roses exploded out of the LA rock scene because their music was raw, uncontrived and savage. Their glam image was certainly designed to appeal to corporate scouts hunting the next Ratt or

Motley Crue, but when *Appetite For Destruction* emerged, angry and wild, no one could have predicted that so real and unrestrained an album could sell so heavily in the notoriously conservative US market.

'Sweet Child O' Mine', W. Axl Rose's heartfelt poem to his future wife Erin Everley that hit the Number 1 position in the US singles chart, would not prepare the casual listener for the war-like intensity of the rest of *Appetite For Desctruction*.

Opening with 'Welcome To The Jungle', GN'R's savage song for Los Angeles, *Appetite For Destruction* careers along on Slash and Izzy's riffs. The new toxic twins fire up some scalding rock 'n' roll; 'Rocket Queen' shreds while 'It's So Easy' is a rebellious slap across the face, hitting hardest when Axl sneers: "Why don't you just fuck off." GN'R may have been ignorant street brats, but they attacked like muggers.

Nor did they ignore the state of themselves. 'Mr Brownstone' is a hazy look at the life of a smack user, and was undoubtedly based on the ordeal the band were going through.

Appetite For Destruction's abandoned attack has spawned myriad wannabes, but its fire and rage have yet to be matched.

IRON MAIDEN

IRON MAIDEN
EMI, 1980

WHEN IRON MAIDEN REPLACED SINGER PAUL DI'ANNO WITH BRUCE "BRUCE" DICKINSON, UK ROCK WRITERS SPOKE NO MORE OF the band's so-called "punk edge". Steve Harris, Maiden's driving force, bass player and chief songwriter, was delighted. With Dickinson, Iron Maiden became the complete traditional British heavy metal band, made Number 1 albums and played marathon sell-out tours; but they never made another album as good as their first.

Di'Anno now admits he might have taken the job a little too lightly, but his phlegmy vocals gave Maiden a street toughness they've since lacked. The band had risen to prominence at the head of the NWOBHM, when headbangers took inspiration from the punk years by cutting records on small budgets for independent labels. The NWOBHM was a grass roots phenomenon, and Iron Maiden, from London's notoriously hard East End, sounded the meanest of the new breed. Di'Anno's snarling made the urgency of 'Running Free' and the menace of 'Prowler' wholly convincing.

Steve Harris believes Will Malone's raw production on *Iron Maiden* weakened a powerful set of songs, yet Maiden have never again sounded so sharp and aggressive. Even the epic 'Phantom Of The Opera' is ferocious where later Maiden period pieces like 'Rime Of The Ancient Mariner' have plodded. As its title suggests, 'Charlotte The Harlot' is the only weak track on the album. The ballad 'Strange World' and the piledriving 'Transylvania' are as strong as established Maiden classics 'Remember Tomorrow' and the signature 'Iron Maiden'.

More so than Saxon's *Wheels Of Steel* or Def Leppard's *On Through the Night, Iron Maiden* is the definitive NWOBHM album, by the band who would evolve into the most successful straight metal act of the Eighties.

JANE'S ADDICTION

RITUAL DE LO HABITUAL
WARNER BROS, 1990

J ANE'S ADDICTION DID NO WRONG IN THEIR 5 YEARS TOGETHER. ECLECTIC, CUTTING AND REVELLING IN CONTROVERSY, they split as superstardom loomed.

Ritual De Lo Habitual, the Los Angeles quartet's third and final album, proved that Jane's Addiction's lofty artistic sensibilities could be married to punk ethics.

Vocalist Perry Farrell, the band's shamanistic leader, was an unlikely anti-hero. Skinny, high-voiced and given to sexual ambiguity over his appearance, he often took the stage in a dress, face pancaked, hair in long ringlets. Where LA's rock bands were ultra-conservative, Jane's Addiction were genuinely threatening and subversive, and open about their enthusiastic use of hard drugs. It was a heady cocktail, Dave Navarro's splintered, spacy riffing

and the jarring rhythms of bassist Eric A and drummer Steven Perkins providing broad vistas on which Perry Farrell could scream his twisted prose.

Ritual De Lo Habitual ran into trouble on its release. Farrell's papier mâché sculpture of a man and two women naked and carressing was reproduced on the front cover and immediately inflamed sensibilities.

'Stop' is a fierce opener, abrasive and hard. Then, in 'Ain't No Right', Farrell offers his motivation: "I am skin and bones/I am pointy nose/but it motherfuckin' makes me try". 'Been Caught Stealing', Farrell's tongue-in-cheek ode to shoplifting, provides light relief.

Ritual De Lo Habitual's centrepiece is 'Three Days', a sparse epic, hypnotic and hallucinogenic and a neat counterpoint to 'Classic Girl', the closest Farrell would get to a conventional love song.

As *Ritual De Lo Habitual's* anarchic brilliance began to catapult the band towards stardom, Farrell decided he could do no more within its constraints, and split the band at its apex.

JOURNEY

RAISED ON RADIO
COLUMBIA, 1986

A MILLION DOLLARS WERE SPENT ON THE RECORDING OF *RAISED ON RADIO*—THE PRICE OF PERFECTION. JOURNEY ARE THE QUINtessential American melodic hard rock act and this, their final work, is surely the ultimate AOR album. The San Franciscans' two previous releases—1981's *Escape* and 1983's *Frontiers*—are both classics, but with *Raised On Radio,* Journey reached their zenith. In particular, the voice of Steve Perry is astounding. Critics said he sounded like a duck, but in the sphere of AOR, Perry has only two serious peers: Lou Gramm of Foreigner and Michael Bolton.

Raised On Radio is in essence Perry's album. He is the album's producer, chief songwriter and star. Having blazed away on the harder-edged *Escape* and *Frontiers,* guitarist and founder member Neal Schon is muzzled on *Raised On Radio,* although he does turn on the power for 'Be Good To Yourself' and the title cut

'Girl Can't Help It' is a stunning opening number, Perry's voice multi-tracked for the chorus and for a wonderful a cappella ending. 'Positive Touch' betrays the group's Sixties soul roots, while 'Suzanne' is one of the most emotive rock songs ever recorded, Perry seemingly on his knees pleading at the finish. Surprisingly, the two ballads, 'Happy To Give' and 'Why Can't This Night Go On Forever', are not among Journey's best. 'Faithfully' remains their classic tearjerker, but *Raised On Radio* is the classic Journey album.

JUDAS PRIEST

UNLEASHED IN THE EAST
CBS, 1979

M OST LIVE ALBUMS ARE OVER DUBBED A LITTLE, AND *UNLEASHED IN THE EAST* IS NO EXCEPTION. IT IS IN FACT SO POLished that critics have mockingly rechristened it *Unleashed In The Studio*! However, while its authenticity as a live recording has been questioned, there is no doubting *Unleashed In The East*'s standing as a classic heavy metal album. Judas Priest are the very epitome of heavy metal and *Unleashed In The East* dates from their golden era, recorded on their 1978 tour of Japan.

'Exciter' is a supremely overstated opening track, off at a gallop, guitars duelling, Rob Halford howling, ranting, squealing: "Fall to your knees and repent if you please!" 'Sinner' is Priest's greatest epic, featuring Halford at his most comically cod-operatic. The singer later adopts the guise of the "Ripper" ("I'm a nasty surprise!") in a dubious ode to the Victorian butcher.

Without mercy, Priest cover Joan Baez ('Diamonds And Rust') and Fleetwood Mac ('The Green Manalishi'). They finish with their own, bloody 'Tyrant', a sabre-rattling Halford leading a merry wardance: "Slice to the left, slice to the right!"

Unleashed In The East is arguably the definitive traditional heavy metal album, bludgeoning yet hi-tech and high-camp, a gothic pantomime, uproarious and overwhelmingly male. If Judas Priest have a feminine side, they weren't in touch with it in 1978! *Unleashed In The East* was Judas Priest's deification.

KING'S X

OUT OF THE SILENT PLANET
MEGAFORCE/ATLANTIC, 1987

THE RELATIVE LACK OF COMMERCIAL SUCCESS ACHIEVED BY *OUT OF THE SILENT PLANET*—THE TEXAN POWER-TRIO KING'S X'S groundbreaking début—should in no way detract from its status. Hearing it is like opening an old door into a summer garden.

The Houston-based three-piece marry sweet harmony vocals on to huge and brutal riffs. Opener 'In The New Age' is a giant statement of intent, and it's followed by 'Goldilox', a pure ballad that retains its gentle theme in the face of the crushing powerchords that fuel it.

King's X—bassist and vocalist Doug Pinnick, guitarist and vocalist Ty Tabor and drummer Jerry Gaskill—are guarded about the band's origins, admitting to little more than a long stretch on the gruelling US bar-band circuit honing their unique brand of spiritual music.

Out Of The Silent Planet was a revelation, a landmark for new and clear-thinking talent. King's X sounded like nobody else; they had Black Sabbath's penchant for an enormo-riff, they could shred like Metallica, they could inspire like U2 and they could sing gospel harmonies straight out of church.

'Visions' is remorseless and crushing, 'Power Of Love' grinds, 'What Is This' gives full range to Pinnick's soulful roar, but it's the sonic directness of 'King' that stands out; 3 minutes of cool, uplifting harmony.

Out Of The Silent Planet has proved hard for King's X to follow. Their subsequent releases remain in the shadow of this giant début.

KISS

ALIVE II
CASABLANCA, 1978

WHEN KISS UNMASKED IN 1983, WIPING AWAY THE GREASEPAINT FOR THE LAST TIME AND ABANDONING THE GREATEST image in rock history, they became just another heavy metal band, and not even a pretty one. Five years previously, when *Alive II* was released, the New Yorkers were godheads, the ultimate teenage rock 'n' roll fantasy.

On this monstrous double live album, the four cartoonish Kiss characters come alive. Starchild Paul Stanley (guitar, vocals) is cheerleader, working a hysterical crowd with an insatiable energy and hilarious raps like, "Everyone's got rock 'n' roll pneumonia, so let's call out Dr Love!!" God of thunder Gene Simmons (bass, vocals) is simply terrifying, a lumbering, armour plated, bat-winged vision from hell, breathing fire and and dribbling blood off the tip of a darting, slithering 7-inch tongue. Drummer Peter Criss, "The Cat", takes centre stage for the syrupy 'Beth', while Space Ace Frehley isn't the world's greatest guitarist, but hell, did Eric Clapton's guitar ever fire rockets?!

And the music? Kiss were the ultimate all-American bubblegum metal band, and *Alive II* includes many of their greatest anthems; 'Shout It Out Loud', 'Love Gun' and 'Detroit Rock City', the latter a tribute to the city that first took Kiss to its heart.

Alive II confirmed that, if not the hottest band in the world as they claimed, Kiss were still the greatest show on earth.

LED ZEPPELIN

PHYSICAL GRAFFTI

SWANSONG, 1975

THE 13 YEARS SINCE LED ZEPPELIN SPLIT—FOLLOWING THE DRINK-INSPIRED DEATH OF THEIR BIG-HEARTED DRUMMER JOHN Bonham—have only enhanced their status. Zeppelin did it all faster, bigger and better than anybody else; they sold more records than anybody else, made more money than anybody else, played bigger, longer shows than anybody else, had a private jet before anybody else and have been imitated, written about and talked about more than anybody else.

Physical Graffiti celebrates that Zeppelin ethos; it's a double album of depth and passion and daring variety. The band ducked from 'In The Light' to 'Down By The Seaside' to 'Trampled Underfoot' without apparent effort.

Page's obsession with Eastern music produced *Physical Graffiti's* greatest—and most replicated—epic, 'Kashmir', with Plant producing a sonic wail to match the guitarist's mesmerizing riff. 'Custard Pie' was brazen fun and 'Black Country Woman' was Plant's paean to the UK's Midlands womanhood.

Physical Graffiti was excessive in every aspect. Zeppelin dared to think big and took it from there, and no one has caught them yet.

METALLICA

RIDE THE LIGHTNING

VERTIGO, 1984

BEFITTING THEIR NAME, METALLICA ARE THE QUINTESSENTIAL NINETIES METAL BAND, AND ONE OF THE MOST SUCcessful. The San Franciscans' latest album, eponymously titled, has sold over 5 million units in the US alone. This is by far their biggest seller, but each of the quartet's five albums have been influential. *Ride The Lightning* is simply the strongest.

With their début album *Kill 'Em All,* Metallica gave the gathering thrash metal movement a focus. With *Ride The Lightning* they made the new sub-genre credible and acceptable to the wider mainstream metal audience. *Ride The Lightning* was the first mature thrash record: song-based, technically skilled, well-produced. And, crucially, it still retained the basic power and high-speed energy of classic thrash.

'Fight Fire With Fire' and 'Trapped Under Ice' are the full-on thrashers, real white-knuckle rides on which Lars Ulrich's snare drum takes a terrible beating. And the slower tracks are even more intense.

Metallica drop a gear on the album's choppy title track and on the biblical epic 'Creeping Death', the latter's riff evoking seminal though ill-fated NWOBHM stars Diamond Head. 'For Whom The Bell Tolls', inspired by the Ernest Hemingway novel, has a booming slow-motion riff heavier than a drowning man. 'The Call Of Ktulu' is a weird, extended instrumental built around the late Cliff Burton's growling bass line. 'Fade To Black' is the first thrash power-ballad, its grim lyric pro-euthanasia like Judas Priest's 'Beyond The Realms Of Death', while at the other extreme, 'Escape' is as close as Metallica will ever get to catchy FM rock.

If *Kill 'Em All* was a blast, all speed-buzz and raw aggression, *Ride The Lightning* is classically-styled post-punk heavy metal. It is Metallica's definitive work.

MOTORHEAD

NO SLEEP TILL HAMMERSMITH

BRONZE, 1981

IN THEIR HEYDAY—BEFORE THRASH METAL REDEFINED THE EXTREMITIES OF MUSIC— MOTORHEAD WERE AN AURAL NAIL bomb, incendiary and deafening. *No Sleep Till Hammersmith,* recorded, obviously enough, at London's metal Valhalla, Hammersmith Odeon, is a wild and raucous celebration of their bludgeoning rock 'n' roll.

Motorhead had built their career on the strength of their live shows since former Hawkwind bassist and vocalist Ian 'Lemmy' Kilmister had put the band together and named it after the last song he wrote for his psychedelic space-cadet employers.

With the classic three-piece line-up established after the recruiting of guitarist "Fast" Eddie Clarke and drummer Phil "Philthy Animal" Taylor, Motorhead transferred their sim-plistic, overdriven rock 'n' roll

tunes on to vinyl without losing their live venom. When they released the pounding 'Ace Of Spades' in 1980, Motorhead were established as one of the top-drawing acts in the UK.

With a sell-out tour culminating at the Hammersmith Odeon, the band ripped into a savage show that retained all of its guts and humour on tape.

Motorhead crash into 'Ace Of Spades', Lemmy's trademark growl and omni-present bass swept along by Philthy's manic drumming. Despite his "Fast" Eddie nickname, Clarke was no Eddie Van Halen, but his blues-led riffing had the fire of belief. 'We Are The Road Crew' cheerfully removes faces.

Those not yet hammered flat by the wall of sound would do well to stand up to the final body-blows, 'Bomber' and 'Motorhead'. Big, fast, dumb and life-threatening, the bikers on the M1 probably felt the vibrations in their sprockets.

Lemmy, man of the rocking peo-ple, had his moments in the sun, and, judging by the vigour of *No Sleep Till Hammersmith,* relished them.

NIRVANA

NEVERMIND
GEFFEN, 1991

THE RAPID AND HUGE COM
MERCIAL SUCCESS OF
NEVERMIND CUT AGAINST THE
GRAIN FOR NIRVANA, THE PUNK-
inspired three-piece from upstate
Washington.

Nirvana gleefully embrace punk
rock sensibilities—casual nihilism
and swearing on television are, it
seems, *de rigueur*—but no punk
band wrote a song as good as
'Smells Like Teen Spirit', *Nevermind's*
outstanding track.

The band spearhead the Seattle
scene that produced Mudhoney,
Soundgarden, the Melvins, Screaming Trees, Mother Love Bone, Pearl
Jam and myriad wannabes. While
grunge metal acts as a generic term
for the Seattle bands, and certainly
sums up Nirvana's noise-fest of a first
album, *Bleach,* for the seminal
SubPop label, *Nevermind's* songs are
as much pop as punk.

Nevermind is suitably spiky and
enraged; vocalist and guitarist
Kurt Cobain produces a grating
rasp to match his fierce playing,
backed by Chris Noveselic's supple
bass and Dave Grohl's harsh percussion. Butch Vig's dry production
adds to the intensity Nirvana whip
up via the tracks 'Territorial Pissings'
and 'Polly'.

However much the delinquent
Cobain wants to be the Sex Pistols,
though, Nirvana cut deeper than
mere delinquent fury allows. 'Come

As You Are',
'Lithium' and 'In
Bloom' are as
well-built as they
are raw, with
neat pop chorus-
es bludgeoned
out with some
brazen playing.

Nevermind is a
unique combina-
tion of anger and
finesse, and
Nirvana, and
e s p e c i a l l y
Cobain, dis-
claimed it the more it sold. They
never wanted it to grow this big,
they announced; Nirvana wasn't
built for corporate stardom. The follow-up, they promise, will be a
return to the white-noise of *Bleach*
and their roots.

Cobain, though, opted for the
celebrity marriage—to his female
equivalent, Hole's Courtney Love—
and naturally, more sales-fuelling
publicity arrived with their first
child, Frances Bean. Nirvana can't
cop out now.

SEX PISTOLS

NEVER MIND THE BOLLOCKS, HERE'S THE SEX PISTOLS
VIRGIN, 1977

BY THE TIME *NEVER MIND THE BOLLOCKS, HERE'S THE SEX PISTOLS* WAS RELEASED, ON OCTOBER 28, 1977, THE SEX Pistols had already carved their way into the nation's psyche in a way no band has duplicated since.

The Pistols were gleefully anti-social; their goals were to discredit the lumbering rock dinosaurs of the 1970s, and to make rock 'n' roll exciting again. Corporate rock, of course, rolls on regardless, but the Pistols, under their cunning svengali Malcolm McLaren, were euphorically exciting.

When *Never Mind The Bollocks* was finally released, the Pistols were already on their third label. EMI had managed to release the 'Anarchy In The UK' single before bowing to increasing controversy, and A&M's week-long and fruitless flirtation with the Pistols had cost them £75,000 ($112,500) before Virgin stepped in. The band were also on their second bassist, having fired Glen Matlock. In his place came Sid Vicious, punk rock embodied, a self-destructive, pale-faced boy, yobbish to the extreme and wearing the look of the doomed.

When the Pistols' second single, 'God Save The Queen', hit Number 2 in the UK singles chart, anticipation over the band's début album reached fever-pitch.

Never Mind The Bollocks lived down to all expectations. The band's first single, 'Anarchy In The UK', provided the blueprint for the brattish 'Holidays In The Sun', and the dumb self-appraisal of 'Pretty Vacant'. The sound of *Never Mind The Bollocks* was a raw cocktail of Steve Jones's deceptively well-crafted and catchy riffs, Johnny Rotten's sneering vocal evocation of the punk ethic and Sid's obnoxious personality.

The album has fuelled a generation. But the Pistols may be best summed up by the title of a retrospective compilation, *It Seemed Like The End Until The Next Beginning.*

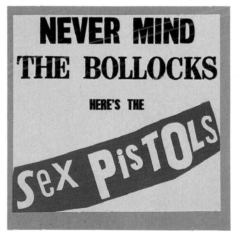

SLAYER

REIGN IN BLOOD
DEF JAM, 1987

REIGN IN BLOOD IS THE ALBUM YOUR PARENTS WARNED YOU ABOUT. IT IS 26 MINUTES OF UNRELENTING HORROR, REMORSELESS and savage, and if it was any longer it would be impossible to listen to.

With *Reign In Blood,* the Los Angeles quartet pushed out the parameters of music, producing a manic intensity that was brutal and disturbing.

Slayer had written 30 minutes of material for *Reign In Blood,* but they played so frenziedly, it was cut in 26 and Def Jam supremo and street guru Rick Rubin somehow harnessed it on to tape.

Controversy erupted immediately over the album's repugnant first track, 'Angel Of Death', an unremittingly grim paean to Nazi war criminal Josef Mengele, which opened with the lyric, "Auschwitz, the meaning of pain".

Def Jam's UK distributors refused to handle the album, which eventually emerged through London Records.

Such is the full-bore madness of *Reign In Blood's* second side, that it's not until 'Raining Blood', the final track, that any song lasts longer than 3 minutes; the relentless 'Necrophobic' is over and gone in 1 minute 38 seconds.

Despite its speed, *Reign In Blood* is performed with remarkable precision. Dave Lombardo's drums rattle like machine guns, the guitars of Kerry King and Jeff Hanneman are meshed together, sick twins, and Tom Araya screams and roars on top of it all. It is remarkable and sinister, an aural car crash, an excercise in madness and excess.

Slayer showed little remorse at the outcry over *Reign In Blood* and 'Angel Of Death' in particular, and the controversy the album generated only added to their mystique. They remain death metal's most extreme arbiters and the only band in that sphere who can boast real commercial appeal. Death sells.

THIN LIZZY

LIVE AND DANGEROUS
VERTIGO, 1978

IN BLACK IRISHMAN PHIL LYNOTT, THIN LIZZY HAD ONE OF ROCK'S FINEST SONGWRITERS. THE BAND ALSO FEATURED, OVER a decade and a half, some of rock's finest guitarists, beginning with Eric Bell (whose lead playing on *Whiskey In The Jar* is some of the most distinctive in rock history) and ending with John Sykes, who added a little steel to Lizzy's final studio album, *Thunder And Lightning*.

Gary Moore also starred briefly in Thin Lizzy—twice!--but the most celebrated of the band's many guitarist partnerships was that of Scott Gorham and Brian Robertson. Among the two or three greatest live hard rock albums ever released, *Live And Dangerous* features American Gorham and Scotsman Robertson, plus Irishmen Lynott and Downey; the classic Thin Lizzy line-up.

Most classic rock albums have two or three great songs, perhaps even five. *Live And Dangerous* has around a dozen. *Jailbreak* was Lizzy's watershed studio recording and is represented here by its title track (a glorious opening number), the romantic 'Cowboy Song', the swash-buckling 'Emerald' and of course the band's biggest hit 'The Boys Are Back In Town', a Saturday night special that's on every good jukebox in the world.

'Don't Believe A Word' and Bob Seger's 'Rosalie' are typically stylish hard rockers, while 'Johnny The Fox Meets Jimmy The Weed' is a funky underworld tale, Lynott revelling in its sleaze. 'Southbound' is a beautiful, lazy drifter's song, and 'Still In Love With You' is the most emotive song Thin Lizzy ever recorded, wherein Lynott just lets his guitarists do most of the talking.

Live And Dangerous was Thin Lizzy's zenith. Eight years after its release, Phil Lynott died from the complications of sustained drug use. He will be remembered as one of rock's great characters.

VAN HALEN

VAN HALEN
WARNER BROTHERS, 1978

THE FIRST VAN HALEN ALBUM DID FOR ROCK GUITAR PLAYING IN THE LATE SEVENTIES WHAT JIMI HENDRIX'S *ARE YOU EXPERIENCED?* did in the late Sixties. Edward Van Halen's "hammer-on" technique, with which he used both hands on the fretboard simultaneously, revolutionized the sound of heavy metal's primary instrument.

Edward's guitar playing also takes centre stage on Van Halen's début, no mean feat considering the overwhelming persona of the group's singer David Lee Roth, surely the greatest showman and rock star of his generation.

Van Halen is one of the most explosive rock 'n' roll records ever released. It begins with a siren—a sample of the band's car horns!—before Edward leads into the first of many heavyweight riffs on 'Runnin' With The Devil', a classic example of swaggering American hard rock. The second track, 'Eruption', is the guitarist's showpiece. More than a decade on, 'Eruption' remains the ultimate exhibition of guitar pyrotechnics.

Although their own material is strong, Van Halen always loved covering rock standards and the occasional off-the-wall number. Here, the two covers are the Kinks' 'You Really Got Me' (widely acknowledged as the first ever metal tune) and John Brim's feelgood rock 'n' roller 'Ice Cream Man'. Both are supercharged almost to the point of overkill, Roth all raspy yelps, Edward roaring yet playful.

Of the band originals, 'Ain't Talkin' 'Bout Love' is arguably the finest song Van Halen have written, 'Atomic Punk' is pure freewheeling energy, while the sly riff to 'Jamie's Cryin'' was to resurface in 1990 as the meat of Tone Loc's 'Wild Thing'.

Van Halen went on to become America's party band in the Eighties, but in a dazzling career, they never really topped this outrageous début.

CDlistings

The following list contains the main releases by the artists and bands described earlier in the book. The artists and bands are listed alphabetically, followed by their albums (also in alphabetical order). Each entry contains the name of the album and the year of original release, followed by the record labels and catalogue numbers under which the albums have been released in CD format, both in the USA and the UK.

Some albums are currently unavailable on CD.

AC/DC

Back In Black *1980*
UK: ATLANTIC K258735
US: ATLANTIC 16018-2

Blow Up Your Video *1988*
UK: ATLANTIC 781828-2

Dirty Deeds Done Dirt Cheap *1976*
UK: ATCO K250323

Flick Of The Switch *1983*
UK: ATLANTIC K7801K7801002

Fly On The Wall *1985*
UK: ATLANTIC K7812632
US: ATLANTIC 81263-2

For Those About To Rock *1981*
UK: ATLANTIC K25085

High Voltage *1975*
UK: ATCO K250257
US: ATLANTIC 36142-2

Highway To Hell *1979*
UK: ATLANTIC K250628

If You Want Blood *1978*
UK: ATLANTIC K785532

Let There Be Rock *1977*
UK: ATLANTIC K250366

Live *1992*
UK: ATCO 7567-92212-2

Powerage *1978*
UK: ATLANTIC K7815482

The Razors Edge

1990
UK: ATCO 7567 9141-2
US: ATLANTIC 91413-2

Who Made Who *1986*
UK: COLUMBIA K7816502
US: ATLANTIC 81650-2

BRYAN ADAMS

Bryan Adams *1980*
UK: A&M CDA3100
US: A&M CD69902

Cuts Like A Knife *1983*
UK: A&M CDA 4919
US: A&M CD69981

Into The Fire *1987*
UK: A&M CDA 3907
US: A&M VPCD-6907

Reckless *1985*
UK: A&M CDA 5013
US: A&M CD5013

Waking Up The Neighbours *1991*
UK: A&M 397164-2
US: A&M CD5367

You Want It You Got It *1981*
UK: A&M CDA 3154
US: A&M CD69955

AEROSMITH

Aerosmith *1973*
UK: COLUMBIA CK 32005

Classics Live *1986*
UK: COLUMBIA

Classics Live II *1987*
UK: COLUMBIA 4600372
US: COLUMBIA 40855

Done With Mirrors *1985*
UK: GEFFEN 924091 2

US: GEFFEN GEFD-24091

Draw The Line *1977*
UK: COLUMBIA CK 34856

Get Your Wings *1974*
UK: COLUMBIA 4667322
US: COLUMBIA 32847

Night In The Ruts *1979*
UK: COLUMBIA CK 36050

Pandora's Box *1992*
UK: COLUMBIA COL 469293-2
US: SONY MUSIC 46209

Permanent Vacation *1987*
UK: GEFFEN 924 162-2
US: GEFFEN GEFD-24162

Pump *1989*
UK: GEFFEN 2-24269
US: GEFFEN GEFD-24254

Rock In A Hard Place *1982*
UK: COLUMBIA CK 38061
US: COLUMBIA CK 38061

Rocks *1976*
UK: COLUMBIA CK 34165

Toys In The Attic *1975*
UK: COLUMBIA CK 33479

ALICE IN CHAINS

Dirt *1992*
UK: COLUMBIA 472330 2

Facelift *1990*
UK: COLUMBIA 4672012
US: COLUMBIA 46075

THE ALMIGHTY

Blood, Fire and Love *1989*
UK: POLYDOR 841347-2
US: POLYGRAM 841347-2

Blood, Fire

---

and Live *1990*
UK: POLYDOR 8471072

Soul Destruction *1991*
UK: POLYDOR 847 961-2
US: POLYGRAM 847961-2

ANTHRAX

Among The Living/Persistence Of Time *1987/1990*
UK: ISLAND 842447-2/POLYGRAM 846480-2

Attack Of The Killer Bs *1991*
UK: ISLAND CID-9980
US: POLYGRAM 848804-2

Fistful Of Metal *1983*
UK: MUSIC FOR NATIONS MFN CDMFN-14
US: CAROLINE 1383

Spreading The Disease *1985*
UK: ISLAND IMCD 136
US: POLYGRAM 826668-2

State Of Euphoria *1988*
UK: MEGAFORCE CID-9916
US: ISLAND 842363-2

BAD COMPANY

Bad Company *1974*
UK: SWAN SONG 7567903332

Desolation Angels *1979*
UK: SWAN SONG 7567903362

Run With The Pack *1976*
UK: SWAN SONG

7567903342
Straight Shooter *1975*
UK: SWAN SONG
7567903322
US: ATLANTIC 8502-2

THE BLACK CROWES
Shake Your Money Maker *1990*
UK: DEF AMERICAN 842 515-2
US: WARNER 26976-2
The Southern Harmony And Musical Companion *1992*
UK: DEF AMERICAN 512 263-2
US: WARNER 26976-2

BLACK SABBATH
Black Sabbath *1970*
UK: CASTLE CLACD 196
Born Again *1983*
UK: VERTIGO 8142712
Dehumanizer *1992*
UK: IRS CDP 7131552
US: WARNER 26965-2
The Eternal Idol *1987*
UK: VERTIGO: VERH
US: WARNER BROS 25548 2
Headless Cross *1990*
UK: IRS EIRSACD1002
US: IRS RECS X21Y-13002
Heaven And Hell *1980*
UK: VERTIGO 8301712
Live Evil *1983*
UK: VERTIGO 8268812
Master Of Reality *1971*
UK: CASTLE CLACD-198

Mob Rules *1981*
UK: VERTIGO 8307777
Never Say Die *1978*
UK: VERTIGO 8307892
Paranoid *1970*
UK: CASTLE CLACD-197
Sabbath Bloody Sabbath *1973*
UK: CASTLE CLACD-201
Sabotage *1975*
UK: CASTLE CLACD-202
Technical Ecstasy *1976*
UK: VERTIGO 8382242
Tyr *1990*
UK: IRS EIRSACD1038
Volume 4 *1972*
UK: CASTLE CLACD-199

BLUE CHEER
Vincebus Eruptum *1968*
UK/US: UNAVAILABLE

BLUE OYSTER CULT
Agents Of Fortune *1976*
UK: COLUMBIA CD-32221
Blue Oyster Cult *1971*
UK: CASTLE CLACD-269
Club Ninja *1985*
UK: COLUMBIA CDCBS-26776
Extra-terrestrial Live *1982*
US: COLUMBIA 37946
Imaginos *1988*
UK: CBS 460036-2
On Your Feet Or On Your Knees *1975*
US: COLUMBIA 33371
Spectres *1977*

UK: CBS CD-82371

BODY COUNT
Body Count *1992*
UK: SIRE 7599-26878-2
US: WARNER 45124-2

BON JOVI
7800 Fahrenheit *1985*
UK: POLYGRAM 8245092
Bon Jovi *1984*
UK: POLYGRAM 8149822
Keep The Faith *1992*
UK: JAMBCO/VERTIGO 514 197 2
New Jersey *1988*
UK: POLYGRAM 836345-2
US: POLYGRAM 836345-2
Slippery When Wet *1986*
UK: POLYGRAM 830264-2
US: POLYGRAM 830264-2

BOSTON
Boston *1976*
UK: CBS: MD81611
US: EPIC 34188
Don't Look Back *1978*
UK: CBS 4032048
US: EPIC 35050
Third Stage *1986*
MCA
UK: MCA DMCG-6017
US: MCA MCAD-6188

BUDGIE
The Best Of *1990*
UK: MCA MCLD 19067
Budgie *1971*
US: ROADRACER 9309
Squawk *1972*

UK: MCA DMCL 1901

BURNING TREE
Burning Tree *1990*
UK: EPIC 466633 2

CELTIC FROST
Cold Lake *1989*
UK: NOISE CDNUK 125
US: NOISE 4803-2
Into The Pandemonium *1987*
UK: NOISE NCD 0067
US: NOISE 44842-2
Morbid Tales/Emperors Return *1984/1983*
UK: NOISE NCD 003
Parched With Thirst Am I And Dying *1991*
UK: NOISE N 191-2
US: NOISE 44852-2
To Mega Therion *1985*
UK: NOISE INID031-3
US: NOISE 44841-2
Vanity/Nemesis *1990*
UK: NOISE 564-7 94070

CHEAP TRICK
All Shook Up *1980*
UK: EPIC
US: EPIC 364948
At Budokan *1978*
UK: EPIC CDEPC-8683
Busted *1990*
UK: SONY MUSIC 466876-2
US: EPIC 46013
The Doctor *1987*
UK: EPIC
Lap Of Luxury *1988*

UK: EPIC 460782-2
US: EPIC 40922

CINDERELLA
Heartbreak Station *1990*
UK: VERTIGO 848018-2
US: POLYGRAM 848018-2
Long Cold Winter *1988*
UK: VERTIGO 834612-2
US: POLYGRAM 834612-2

ALICE COOPER
Alice Cooper Goes To Hell *1976*
UK: WEA 7599272992
US: WARNER BKYS CD 02896
Billion Dollar Babies *1973*
UK: WEA 759927692
US: WARNER BROS CD-02685
Constrictor *1986*
UK: MCA DMLF-3341
US: MCA MCAD-5761
Easy Action *1970*
US: RHINE 70350-2
Hey Stoopid *1991*
UK: EPIC: 4684162
US: SONY MUSIC 46786
Killer *1971*
UK: WARNER BROS 927255-2
Ladies Man *1987*
UK: THUNDERBOLT CDTB-090
US: MAGNUM 90
Pretties For You *1969*
US: RHINO 70351-2
Raise Your Fist And Yell *1987*
UK: MCA DMCF-3392
US: MCA MCAD-42091

School's Out *1971*
UK: WARNER BROS 927260-2
Trash *1989*
UK: EPIC 4651302

THE CULT
Ceremony *1991*
UK: BEGGARS BANQUET
BEGA122
Dreamtime *1983*
UK: BEGGARS BANQUET
BBL57CD
US: BEGGARS BANQUET BQ57
Electric *1987*
UK: BEGGARS BANQUET
BEGA 80
Love *1985*
UK: BEGGARS BANQUET
BEGA 65
Pure Cult *1993*
UK: BEGGARS BANQUET
BEGA130
Sonic Temple *1989*
UK: BEGGARS BANQUET
BEGA 98

DANZIG
Danzig *1988*
US: WARNER BROS 24208-2
Danzig II: Lucifuge
1990
US: WARNER BROS 24281-2
**Danzig III: How
The Gods Kill** *1992*
UK: DEF AMERICAN 512270-2
US: WARNER BROS 26914-2

DEEP PURPLE
The Anthology *1985*
UK: EMI CDEM 1374
**The Best Of Deep
Purple** *1990*

UK: EMI: CDFA 3239
**The Book Of
Taliesyn** *1969*
UK: EMI HARVEST CDP
792408-2
Burn *1974*
UK: EMI CZ 203
US: DEEP PURPLE 2766-2
**Come Taste The
Band** *1975*
UK: EMI CDP7940322
US: WARNER BROS 26454-2
**Concerto For Group
And Orchestra** *1970*
UK: HARVEST CDP 7948862
Deep Purple *1969*
UK: HARVEST C2-172
**Deep Purple In
Concert** *1980*
UK: HARVEST CDS 798 1812
**Deep Purple In
Rock** *1970*
UK: EMI CDFA 3011
US: WARNER BROS 01877
Fireball *1971*
UK: EMI CZ 30
US: DEEP PURPLE 2564-2
**House Of Blue
Light** *1987*
UK: POLYDOR 8313182
Machine Head *1971*
UK: EMI CDFA 3158
US: WARNER BROS 03100
Made In Europe
1976
UK: EMI CDP 7937962
Made In Japan *1972*
UK: HARVEST CDFA 3268
Nobody's Perfect
1988
UK: POLYDOR 835897-2
US: POLYGRAM 834897-2

Perfect Strangers
1984
UK: POLYDOR 823777-2
Scandinavian Nights
1988
UK: CONNOISSEUR CONN EU
DPVSOP CD-125
**Shades Of Deep
Purple** *1968*
UK: EMI CZ 170
Slaves And Masters
1990
UK: BMG PD90535
Stormbringer *1974*
UK: EMI CZ 142
US: WARNER BROS 26456-2
**Who Do We Think
We Are** *1973*
UK: EMI CZ 6
US: DEEP PURPLE 2678-2

DEF LEPPARD
Adrenalize *1992*
UK: PHONOGRAM 510978
US: POLYGRAM 512185
High 'N' Dry *1981*
UK: PHONOGRAM 818836-2
US: POLYGRAM 818836-2
Hysteria *1987*
UK: PHONOGRAM 830675-2
US: POLYGRAM 830675-1
**On Through The
Night** *1980*
UK: PHONOGRAM 822533-2
US: POLYGRAM 822533-2
Pyromania *1983*
UK: PHONOGRAM 810308-2
US: POLYGRAM 810308-2

DEICIDE
Deicide *1990*
US: R/C RECS 9381

Legion *1992*
UK: ROADRUNNER
RC RC-9192-2
US: R/C RECS 9192

DIAMOND HEAD
**Behold The
Beginning** *1986*
UK: METAL MASTERS
WKFMXD 92
US: RESTLESS 72200-2

DIO
Diamonds *1992*
UK: VERTIGO: 5122062
Dream Evil *1987*
UK: POLYGRAM 832530-2
Holy Diver *1983*
UK: VERTIGO 8110212
Last In Line *1985*
UK: POLYGRAM 822366-2
Sacred Heart *1986*
UK: POLYGRAM 824848-2

ENUFF ZNUFF
Enuff Znuff *1989*
UK: ATCO 791 262-2
Strength *1991*
UK: ATCO 7567-91638
US: ATLANTIC 91638-2

EUROPE
**The Final
Countdown** *1986*
UK: EPIC 4663282
Out Of This World
1988
UK: EPIC: EPC 462492
**Prisoners In
Paradise**
1991
UK: EPIC 4687552

US: SONY MUSIC 45328

EXODUS
Bonded By Blood
1985
UK: MUSIC FOR NATIONS
MFN 44
US: RELATIVITY 8019-2
Fabulous Disaster
1989
UK: MUSIC FOR NATIONS
MFN 90
Force Of Habit *1992*
UK: CAPITOL CDP 7966762
US: CAPITOL C215-96676
**Good Friendly
Violent Fun** *1990*
UK: ROADRACER RO9235-2
US: RELATIVITY 2026-2

EXTREME
Extreme *1989*
UK: A&M CDA 5238
US: A&M CD 5238
**Extreme II:
Pornograffitti** *1990*
UK: A&M 395 313-2
US: A&M CD 5313

FAITH NO MORE
Angel Dust *1992*
UK: SLASH 8284012
US: WARNER BROS 26785-2
Introduce Yourself
1987
UK: SLASH 82805
US: WARNER BROS 25559-2
The Real Thing *1989*
UK: SLASH 8281542
US: WARNER BROS 25878-2
**You Fat Bastard:
Live At Brixton**

Academy *1990*
UK: SLASH 8282382

FOREIGNER
4 *1981*
UK: ATLANTIC K250796
Agent Provocateur
1984
UK: ATLANTIC K7819992
Double Vision *1978*
UK: ATLANTIC K250476
Foreigner *1977*
UK: ATLANTIC K250356
Inside Information
1988
UK: ATLANTIC K7818082
Unusual Heat *1991*
UK: ATLANTIC 756782299 2
US: ATLANTIC 82299-2

FREE
The Best Of Free
1979
UK: ISLAND CIDTV 2
US: A&M CD 3663
Fire And Water *1970*
UK: ISLAND CID 9104
US: A&M 75021-3663-2
Free At Last *1972*
UK: ISLAND CID 9192
Free Live *1971*
UK: ISLAND CID 9160
US: A&M 75021-4306-2
Heartbreaker *1973*
UK: ISLAND CID 9217
US: POLYGRAM 842361-2
Highway *1971*
UK: ISLAND CID 9138

GIRLSCHOOL
Demolition *1980*
UK: DOJO LOMACD 1

Play Dirty *1983*
UK: DOJO LONACD 4

GUNS N' ROSES
**Appetite For
Destruction** *1987*
UK: GEFFEN 924148-2
US: GEFFEN GEFD 24148
GN'R Lies *1988*
UK: GEFFEN 924198-2
US: GEFFEN GEFD 24198
Use Your Illusion I
1991
UK: GEFFEN GEFD 24415
US: GEFFEN GEFD 24415
Use Your Illusion II
1991
UK: GEFFEN GEFD 24420
US: GEFFEN GEFD 24420

HANOI ROCKS
**All Those Wasted
Years** *1984*
UK: LICK LICCD 3/6
US: GEFFEN GEFD 24266
**Back To Mystery
City** *1983*
UK: LICK LICCD 1
**Self Destruction
Blues** *1982*
UK: LICK LICCD4
US: CAROLINE 1704
**Tracks From A
Broken Dream** *1989*
UK: LICK LICCD10
US: CAROLINE 1704
**Two Steps From The
Move** *1984*
UK: COLUMBIA 4714172

HEART
Bad Animals *1987*

UK: CAPITOL: CDP 7466762
Brigade *1990*
UK: CAPITOL: CDP 7918202
US: CAPITOL C212-91820
Dog And Butterfly
1979
UK: SONY MUSIC CD 32803
Dreamboat Annie
1976
UK: CAPITOL CDP 7464912
US: CAPITOL C21Y 46491
Heart *1985*
UK: CAPITOL CDP 7461572
Little Queen *1977*
UK: PORTRAIT CDPRT 82075
US: PORTRAIT 34799
Magazine *1978*
UK: EMI CZ73
US: CAPITOL C21Y-46492
**Rock The House
Live** *1991*
UK: CAPITOL; CDP 7957977
US: CAPITOL C212-95797

HELLOWEEN
**The Best, The Rest
And The Rare!
1984–88** *1992*
UK: NOISE N01762
US: NOISE 44849-2
Helloween *1985*
UK: NOISE INTERNATIONAL
CDN UK 088
US: NOISE 44847-2
**Keeper Of The
Seven Keys Part I**
1987
UK: NOISE N0061
US: NOISE 6399-2
**Keeper Of The
Seven Keys Part II**
1988

UK: NOISE N0117-3
US: NOISE 8529-2
**Pink Bubbles Go
Ape** *1991*
UK: EMI CDP 7960862
Walls Of Jericho
1986
UK: NOISE N008R
US: NOISE 44847-2

HELMET
Meantime *1991*
UK: INTERSCOPE 7567921622
US: ATLANTIC 92162-2

JIMI HENDRIX
**Are You
Experienced?** *1967*
UK: POLYDOR 825416-2
US: REPRISE RS-06261
Axis, Bold As Love
1968
UK: POLYDOR 8472432
Band Of Gypsies
1970
UK: POLYDOR 8472372
Cornerstones: 67–70
1990
UK: POLYDOR 8472312
Crash Landing *1980*
UK: POLYDOR 8472632
The Cry of Love
1971
UK: POLYDOR 847242-2
US: REPRISE CD-02034
Electric Ladyland
1968
UK: POLYDOR 847233-2
US: REPRISE CD-06307
Isle Of Wight *1971*
UK: POLYDOR 8472362
Kiss The Sky *1984*

UK: POLYDOR: 847261-2
Live At Winterland
1990
UK: POLYDOR 847238-2
Loose Ends *1974*
UK: POLYDOR 837574-2
Midnight Lightning
1975
UK: POLYDOR 825166-2
Radio One Sessions
1989
UK: CASTLE CCSCD 212
US: RYKODISC RCD-20078
Smash Hits *1969*
UK: POLYDOR 825255-2
US: WARNER BROS 2276-2
Stages *1991*
UK: POLYDOR 511763 D
US: WARNER BROS 267 32-2
War Heroes *1972*
UK: POLYDOR 847262-2

IRON MAIDEN
Fear Of The Dark
1992
UK: EMI CDP 7991612
US: SONY MUSIC 48993
Iron Maiden *1980*
UK: EMI CDFA 3121
Killers *1981*
UK: EMI CDFA 3127
Live After Death
1985
UK: EMI CDFA 3248
**No Prayer For The
Dying** *1990*
UK: EMI CDP 7951422
**Number Of The
Beast** *1982*
UK: EMI CDFA 3178
Piece Of Mind *1983*
UK: EMI CDFA 3245

Powerslave *1984*
UK: EMI: CDFA 3244
Seventh Son Of A Seventh Son *1988*
UK: EMI CDFA 3246
Somewhere In Time *1986*
UK: EMI CDFA 3246

JANE'S ADDICTION
Nothing's Shocking *1988*
UK: WARNER BROS 925727-2
US: WARNER BROS 25727-2
Ritual De Lo Habitual *1990*
UK: WARNER BROS 7599-25993-2
US: WARNER BROS 25993-2

JOURNEY
Captured *1981*
UK: COLUMBIA 451132-2
US: COLUMBIA 37016
Departure *1980*
UK: COLUMBIA CD-84101
US: COLUMBIA 36339
Escape *1982*
UK: CBS 4601852
Evolution *1979*
UK: SONY 982737-2
US: COLUMBIA 35797
Greatest Hits *1988*
UK: CBS 4631492
US: COLUMBIA 44493
Raised On Radio *1986*
UK: CBS 4679922

JUDAS PRIEST
British Steel *1980*

UK: SONY 9482725-2
Painkiller *1990*
UK: CBS 4672901
Priest Live *1987*
UK: COLUMBIA 450639-2
US: COLUMBIA 40794
Ram It Down *1988*
UK: COLUMBIA 46118-2
US: COLUMBIA 44244
Rocka Rolla *1974*
UK: LINE LICD 900101
Sad Wings Of Destiny *1976*
UK: LINE LICD 900112
US: RCA 4747-2
Screaming For Vengeance *1982*
UK: SONY MUSIC CD 85941
Stained Class *1978*
UK: CBS CD32075
Turbo *1986*
UK: COLUMBIA 463365-2
Unleashed In The East *1979*
US: COLUMBIA 36179

KINGDOM COME
Hands Of Time *1991*
UK: POLYDOR 849329-2
US: POLYGRAM 849329-2
In Your Face *1989*
UK: POLYDOR 839192-2
US: POLYGRAM 839192-2
Kingdom Come *1988*
UK: POLYDOR 835368-2

KING'S X
Faith Hope Love *1990*
UK: MEGAFORCE 7567-82145-2
US: ATLANTIC 82145-2

King's X *1991*
UK: ATLANTIC 7567805062
US: ATLANTIC 82372-2
Out Of The Silent Planet *1987*
UK: MEGAFORCE 781835-2
US: MEGAFORCE 81825-2

KISS
Alive! *1975*
UK: CASABLANCA 822780-2
US: POLYGRAM 822780-2
Alive II *1977*
UK: CASABLANCA 822781-2
US: POLYGRAM 822781-2
Animalize *1984*
UK: VERTIGO 822 4952
US: UNAVAILABLE
Asylum *1985*
UK: VERTIGO 826099-2
US: POLYGRAM 826099-2
Crazy Nights *1987*
UK: VERTIGO 832 6262
Creatures Of The Night *1982*
UK: CASABLANCA ???
Destroyer *1976*
UK: CASABLANCA 824 1492
Dressed To Kill *1975*
UK: CASABLANCA 824 1482
Hot In The Shade *1989*
UK: VERTIGO 838 9132
US: POLYGRAM 838913-2
Hotter Than Hell *1974*
UK: CASABLANCA 824 1472
Lick It Up *1983*
UK: VERTIGO 824 1462
Revenge *1992*
UK: MERCURY 848 037-2
US: POLYGRAM 848037-2

Unmasked *1980*
UK: CASABLANCA 800 0412
US: POLYGRAM 800041-2

KROKUS
The Blitz *1984*
US: ARISTA ARCD-8243
Headhunter *1983*
UK: ARISTA 255 255
US: ARISTA ARCD-8005

LA GUNS
Cocked And Loaded *1989*
UK: VERTIGO 838 592-2
Hollywood Vampires *1991*
UK: MERCURY 849 604-2
US: POLYGRAM 849485-2
LA Guns *1987*
UK: VERTIGO 834 144-2

LED ZEPPELIN
Coda *1982*
UK: SWAN SONG 7900512
US: SWAN SONG 90051-2
Houses Of The Holy *1973*
UK: ATLANTIC K250074
US: ATLANTIC 19130-2
In Through The Out Door *1979*
UK: SWAN SONG SK259410
US: ATLANTIC CD-16002
Led Zeppelin *1969*
UK: ATLANTIC K240031
US: ATLANTIC 19126-2
Led Zeppelin II *1970*
UK: ATLANTIC K240037
US: ATLANTIC 19127-2
Led Zeppelin III

1970
UK: ATLANTIC K250002
US: ATLANTIC CD-19128
Led Zeppelin IV *1971*
UK: ATLANTIC K250008
Physical Graffiti *1975*
UK: SWAN SONG SK289400
US: ATLANTIC 200-2
Presence *1976*
UK: SWAN SONG SK259402
US: SWAN SONG 8416-2
Remasters *1990*
UK: EASTWEST 7567804152
US: ATLANTIC 82371-2
Remasters II *1993*
UK: EASTWEST 7567821442
The Song Remains The Same *1976*
UK: SWAN SONG: SK28402
US: ATLANTIC CD-00201

LITTLE ANGELS
Don't Prey For Me *1989*
UK: POLYDOR 8434692
US: POLYGRAM 843073-2
Young Gods *1991*
UK: POLYDOR 8478462
US: POLYGRAM 511060-2

LYNYRD SKYNYRD
Gimme Back My Bullets *1976*
UK: MCA MCLD19138
US: MCA MCAD-31004
Nuthin' Fancy *1975*
UK: MCA MCLD19074
US: MCA MCAD-31003
One More From The Road *1976*

UK: MCA MCLD19139
US: MCA MCAD-6897
**Pronounced Leh-
nerd Skin-nerd** *1973*
UK: MCA MCLD19072
US: MCA MCAD-1685
Second Helping
1974
UK: MCA MCLD19073
US: MCA MCAD-1686
Skynyrd's Innyrds
1990
UK: MCA DMCG6046
US: MCA MCAD-42293
**Southern By The
Grace Of God** *1989*
UK: MCA MCLD19010
US: MCA MCAD 8027
Street Survivors
1977
US: MCA MCAD-1687

**YNGWIE J.
MALMSTEEN**
The Collection *1991*
UK: Polydor 8492712
US: Polygram 849271-2
Eclipse *1990*
UK: Polydor 843361-2
US: Polygram 843361-2
Fire And Ice *1991*
UK: WEA 7559611372
US: Elektra 61137-2
Odyssey *1988*
UK: Polydor 8354512
US: Polygram 835451-2

MANOWAR
Kings Of Metal *1988*
UK: WEA 781930-2
US: Atlantic 81930-2

MARILLION
B-Sides Themselves
1988
UK: EMI CDP 7488072
US: Unavailable
Clutching At Straws
1987
UK: EMI CDP 7468662
Fugazi *1984*
UK: EMI CDFA 3196
Holidays In Eden
1991
UK: IRS RECS X21S-13138
**Misplaced
Childhood** *1985*
UK: EMI CDFA 3258
Real To Reel *1984*
UK: EMI CDFA 3412
**Script For A Jester's
Tear** *1983*
UK: EMI CDFA 3235
US: Capitol C21Y-46237
Seasons End *1990*
UK: EMI CDP 7928772
**The Thieving
Magpie** *1988*
UK: EMI CDS 7914632
US: Capitol CZAY-91463

MC5
Kick Out The Jams
1968
UK: Elektra 7559 74042-2

MEAT LOAF
Bad Attitude *1984*
UK: Arista 259049
Bat Out Of Hell
1978
UK: Epic CDX82419
US: Epic 34974

Blind Before I Stop
1986
UK: Arista 257741
Dead Ringer *1981*
UK: Epic CD 83645
Hits Out Of Hell
1989
UK: Epic 4504472
Meat Loaf Live *1987*
UK: Arista 258599
**Midnight At The
Lost And Found**
1983
UK: Epic 4503602

MEGADETH
**Countdown To
Extinction** *1992*
UK: Capitol CDP 7985312
US: Capitol C21Z-98531
**Killing Is My
Business... And
Business Is Good!**
1985
UK: Music For Nations
MFN 46
US: Relativity 8015-2
**Peace Sells... But
Who's Buying?** *1986*
UK: Capitol CDFA 3242
US: Capitol C21Y-46370
Rust In Peace *1990*
UK: Capitol CDP 7919352
US: Capitol C21S-91935
**So Far, So Good, So
What!** *1988*
UK: Capitol CDP 7481482
US: Capitol C21S-48148

METALLICA
**...And Justice For
All**

1988
UK: Vertigo 9 60812-2
US: Elektra 60812-2
Kill 'Em All *1983*
UK: Vertigo 838 142-2
Master Of Puppets
1986
UK: Vertigo 838 141-2
US: Elektra 60439-2
Metallica *1991*
UK: Vertigo 510 022-2
US: Elektra 61113-2
Ride The Lightning
1984
UK: Vertigo 838 140-2
US: Elektra 60396-2

MINISTRY
**Psalm 69: How To
Succeed And Suck
Eggs** *1992*
UK: WEA 7599267272
US: Warner 26727-2

MONTROSE
Montrose *1973*
UK: Warner Bros CD-03106

MOTHER LOVE BONE
Apple *1990*
UK: Polydor 843 192-2
US: Polygram 843191-2

MOTLEY CRUE
**Decade Of
Decadence** *1991*
UK: Elektra 7559612042
US: Elektra 61204-2
Dr Feelgood *1989*
UK: Elektra K9608292
US: Electra 60829-2
Girls Girls Girls *1987*

UK: Elektra K9607252
US: Elektra 60725-2
Shout At The Devil
1983
UK: Elektra K9602892
US: Elektra 60289-2
Theatre Of Pain *1985*
UK: Elektra K9604182
US: Elektra 60418-2

MOTORHEAD
1916 *1991*
UK: Epic 4674812
US: Sony Music 46858
Ace Of Spades *1980*
UK: Castle CLACD 240
US: Roadracer 9227
Another Perfect Day
1983
UK: Castle CLACD-225
Bomber *1978*
UK: Legacy LLMCD-3012
US: Roadracer 9228
Iron Fist *1982*
UK: Bronze CLACD-123
March Or Die *1992*
UK: Epic 4717232
US: Sony Music 48997
Motorhead *1977*
UK: Big Beat CDWIK-2
No Sleep At All *1988*
UK: GWR GWCD-31
US: Roadracer 9514
**No Sleep Till
Hammersmith** *1981*
UK: Legacy CLACD-179
On Parade *1980*
UK: Fame CDFA-3251
US: Cleopatra 57666
Orgasmatron *1986*
UK: Castle CLACD-283
US: Sinclair 1007

137

Overkill 1979
UK: CASTLE CLACD 178
US: ROADRACER 9229
Rock And Roll 1987
US: SINCLAIR 1006

MR BIG
Lean Into It 1991
UK: ATLANTIC: 7567822092
US: ATLANTIC 8209-2
Mr Big 1989
UK: ATLANTIC: K7819902
US: ATLANTIC 81990-2

NAPALM DEATH
**From Enslavement
To Obliteration** 1988
UK: EARACHE MOSH 8-CD
US: RELATIVITY 1066-2
**Harmony
Corruption**
1989
UK: EARACHE MOSH 19CD
US: RELATIVITY 2020-2
Scum 1987
US: RELATIVITY 1065-2

NELSON
After The Rain 1990
UK: GEFFEN 924290-D2
US: GEFFEN GEFD-24290

NIRVANA
Bleach 1989
UK: GEFFEN GED 24433
US: SUBPOP 34
Incesticide 1992
UK: GEFFEN GED 24421
Nevermind 1991
UK: GEFFEN GED 24425
US: GEFFEN GEFD-24425

TED NUGENT
Double Live Gonzo
1978
US: EPIC E2K-35069
**Intensities In 10
Cities**
1981
US: SONY MUSIC 37084
Nugent 1982
US: ATLANTIC 19365-2
State Of Shock 1979
US: SONY MUSIC 36000
**Ted Nugent/Free
For All/Cat Scratch
Fever** 1980
UK: EPIC 4688052
US: EPIC 33692/EPIC
34121/EPIC 34700

OZZY OSBOURNE
Bark At The Moon
1984
UK: EPIC CD32780
Blizzard Of Ozz
1980
UK: EPIC CDJET234
Diary Of A Madman
1981
UK: EPIC 4630862
No More Tears 1992
UK: EPIC 4678592
US: SONY MUSIC 46795
**No Rest For The
Wicked** 1988
UK: SONY MUSIC 462581-2
Talk Of The Devil
1982
UK: CASTLE CCSCD-296
Tribute 1987
UK: EPIC 4504752
US: JET 40714
The Ultimate Sin

1986
UK: EPIC 4624962

PANTERA
Cowboys From Hell
1990
UK: ATLANTIC 7567913722
US: ATLANTIC 91372-2
**A Vulgar Display Of
Power** 1991
UK: ATLANTIC 7567987582
US: ATLANTIC 91758-2

PEARL JAM
Ten 1991
UK: EPIC 468884-2
US: ATLANTIC 91372-2

POISON
Flesh And Blood
1990
UK: CAPITOL CDP 7918132
US: CAPITOL C21Z-91813
**Look What The Cat
Dragged In** 1986
UK: CAPITOL CDP 7467352
US: CAPITOL C21Y-46735
Native Tongue 1993
UK: CAPITOL CDP7-2
**Open Up And Say...
Ahh** 1988
UK: CAPITOL CDP 7484932
US: CAPITOL C21Z-48493
Swallow This Live
1991
UK: CAPITOL CDP7980382
US: CAPITOL C22V-948046

QUEEN
A Day At The Races
1976
UK: EMI CDP 746208-2

US: HOLLYWOOD 61035-2
Flash Gordon 1980
UK: EMI CDP 746214-2
US: HOLLYWOOD 61203-2
The Game 1980
UK: EMI CDP 746213-2
US: HOLLYWOOD 61063-2
Greatest Hits II 1991
UK: PARLOPHONE CDP
797971-2
Hot Space 1981
UK: EMI CDP 746215-2
US: HOLLYWOOD 61038-2
Innuendo 1991
UK: PARLOPHONE CDP
796887-2
US: HOLLYWOOD 61021-2
Jazz 1978
UK: EMI CDP 7462102
US: HOLLYWOOD 61062-2
A Kind Of Magic
1986
UK: EMI CDP 746267-2
US: HOLLYWOOD 61152-2
Live Magic 1988
UK: EMI CDP 746413-2
US: HOLLYWOOD 61066-2
The Miracle 1989
UK: PARLOPHONE CDP
792357-2
US: HOLLYWOOD 61234-2
Live Killers 1979
US: HOLLYWOOD 61066-2
News Of The World
1977
UK: EMI CDP 7462092
US: HOLLYWOOD 61037-2
**A Night At The
Opera** 1975
UK: EMI CDP 7462072
US: HOLLYWOOD 61065-2
Queen I 1973

UK: EMI CDFA 3040
US: HOLLYWOOD 61064-2
Queen II 1974
UK: EMI CDFA 3099
US: HOLLYWOOD 61232-2
Sheer Heart Attack
1974
UK: EMI CDP 7462062
US: HOLLYWOOD 61036-2

QUEENSRYCHE
Empire 1990
UK: EMI CDP 7950692
US: EMI AMERICA E21Z-
92806
**Operation:
Mindcrime** 1988
UK: EMI CDP 7486402
US: EMI AMERICA E21Z-
48640
Rage For Order 1986
UK: EMI CDP 7463302
US: EMI AMERICA E21Z-
46330
The Warning 1984
UK: EMI CDP 746330-2
US: EMI AMERICA E21Z-
46557

QUIREBOYS
**A Bit Of What You
Fancy** 1990
UK: PARLOPHONE CDP
7931772
**Bitter Sweet And
Twisted** 1993
UK: PARLOPHONE CDP
7987972

RAINBOW
Bent Out Of Shape
1983

138

UK: POLYDOR 815305-2
US: POLYGRAM 815305-2

Difficult To Cure
1981
UK: POLYDOR 800018-2
US: POLYGRAM 800018-2

Down To Earth *1979*
UK: POLYDOR 823705-2
US: POLYGRAM 823705-2

Long Live Rock And Roll *1978*
UK: POLYDOR 825090-2
US: POLYGRAM 825090-2

On Stage *1977*
UK: POLYDOR 823656-2
US: POLYGRAM 823656-2

Rising *1976*
UK: POLYDOR 823655-2
US: POLYGRAM 823655-2

Ritchie Blackmore's Rainbow *1975*
UK: POLYDOR 825089-2
US: POLYGRAM 825089-2

Straight Between The Eyes *1982*
UK: POLYDOR 800028-2
US: POLYGRAM 800028-2

RATT

Detonator *1991*
UK: ATLANTIC 7567-82127-2

Ratt 'N' Roll *1991*
US: ATLANTIC 82260-2

Reach For The Sky *1990*
UK: ATLANTIC 781929-2
US: ATLANTIC 818929-2

RED HOT CHILI PEPPERS

Blood Sugar Sex

Magik *1991*
UK: WARNER BROS 7599-26681-2
US: WARNER BROS 26681-2

Freaky Styley *1985*
UK: EMI CDP 7906172
US: EMI AMERICA E21Y-90617

Mother's Milk *1989*
UK: EMI CDP 7921522
US: EMI AMERICA E21Z-92152

The Uplift Mofo Party Plan *1988*
UK: EMI CDP 7480362
US: EMI AMERICA E21Y-48036

DAN REED NETWORK

Dan Reed Network
1988
UK: MERCURY 834309-2
US: POLYGRAM 834309-2

The Heat *1991*
UK: MERCURY 848855-2
US: POLYGRAM 848855-2

Slam *1989*
UK: MERCURY 838868-2
US: POLYGRAM 838868-2

ROSE TATTOO

Assault And Battery
1981
UK: STREETLINK STRCD-3

DAVID LEE ROTH

Crazy From The Heat *1985*
UK: WARNER BROS 7599252222
US: WARNER BROS 25222-2

Eat 'Em And Smile

1986
UK: WARNER BROS K9254702
US: WARNER 25470-2

A Little Ain't Enough *1991*
UK: WARNER BROS 7599264772
US: WARNER BROS K9258242

RUSH

Chronicles *1990*
UK: MERCURY 8389362
US: POLYGRAM 838936-2

Exit Stage Left *1981*
UK: MERCURY 8725512
US: POLYGRAM 822551-2

Grace Under Pressure *1984*
UK: MERCURY 8184762

Hold Your Fire *1987*
UK: MERCURY 8324642

Moving Pictures
1981
UK: MERCURY 8000482

Permanent Waves
1980
UK: MERCURY 8223482

Power Windows
1985
UK: MERCURY 8260982
US: POLYGRAM 826098-2

Presto *1989*
UK: ATLANTIC K7820402

Roll The Bones *1991*
UK: ATLANTIC 7567822932
US: ATLANTIC 82293-2

Signals *1982*
UK: MERCURY 8100022

JOE SATRIANI

The Extremist *1991*

UK: EPIC 471672 2
US: RELATIVITY 1053-2

Flying In A Blue Dream *1989*
UK: FOOD FOR THOUGHT GRUB 9
US: RELATIVITY 1015 2

Not Of This Earth
1987
UK: FOOD FOR THOUGHT GRUB 7
US: RELATIVITY 8110-2

Surfing With The Alien *1988*
UK: FOOD FOR THOUGHT GRUB 8
US: RELATIVITY 8193-2

SAXON

Crusader *1984*
UK: EMI CDFMS 390

Destiny *1988*
UK: EMI CDP 790066-2

The Eagle Has Landed *1982*
UK: EMI CZ210-2

Power And The Glory *1983*
UK: EMI CZ209

Rock 'N' Roll Gypsies *1990*
UK: ENIGMA RR94162

Solid Ball Of Rock
1991
UK: VIRGIN CDVIR-4
US: VIRGIN 91672-2

SCORPIONS

Animal Magnetism
1980
UK: EMI CDFA 3217

Best Of Rockers

And Ballads *1989*
UK: EMI CDFA 3262
US: ISLAND 842002-2

Blackout *1982*
UK: EMI CDFA 3126
US: POLYGRAM 818885 2

Crazy World *1990*
UK: VERTIGO 846908-2
US: POLYGRAM 846908-2

Fly To The Rainbow
1974
UK: RCA ND 70084
US: RCA 5057-2

Love At First Sting
1984
UK: EMI CDFA 3224
US: POLYGRAM 8149481-2

Lovedrive *1979*
UK: EMI CDFA 3080

Savage Amusement
1988
UK: EMI HARVEST CDSHSP-4125
US: POLYGRAM 832963-2

Trance *1976*
UK: RCA ND 70028
US: RCA 4128-7

Virgin Killers *1976*
UK: RCA ND 70031
US: RCA 3659-2

World Wide Live
1985
UK: EMI CDS 7979632

SEPULTURA

Arise *1991*
UK: ROADRUNNER RO9328
US: R/C RECS 9328

Beneath The Remains *1988*
UK: ROADRUNNER RO9511
US: R/C RECS 9511

Morbid Visions *1985*
UK: ROADRUNNER RO9276
US: NEW RENSC 43
Schizophrenia *1986*
UK: ROADRUNNER RO9360
US: R/C RECS 9360

SEX PISTOLS
Never Mind The
Bollocks, Here's The
Sex Pistols *1977*
UK: VIRGIN CDV 2086
US: WARNER BROS 3147-2

SKID ROW
B-Sides Ourselves
1992
UK: ATLANTIC 7567824312
Skid Row *1989*
UK: ATLANTIC K7781936-2
US: ATLANTIC 81936-2
Slave To The Grind
1991
UK: ATLANTIC 7567822422
US: ATLANTIC 82242-2

SLAYER
Decade Of
Aggression *1991*
UK: DEF AMERICAN 510605-2
US: WARNER BROS 26748-2
Hell Awaits *1985*
UK: METAL BLADE ZORRO 8
US: RESTLESS 72297-2
Live Undead *1985*
UK: METAL BLADE ZORRO 29
US: RESTLESS 72217-2
Reign In Blood *1986*
US: DEF JAM 24131-2
Seasons In The
Abyss
1990

UK: DEF AMERICAN 846871-2
US: WARNER BROS 24307-2
Show No Mercy
1984
UK: METAL BLADE ZORRO 7
US: RESTLESS 71034-2
South Of Heaven
1988
UK: DEF AMERICAN 828080-2
US: WARNER BROS 24203-2

SOUNDGARDEN
Badmotorfinger
1991
UK: A&M: 395 374-2
US: A&M CD-5374
Louder Than Love
1989
UK: A&M CDA5252
US: A&M CD5252
Ultramega OK *1987*
US: SST SSTCD-201

STATUS QUO
12 Gold Bars *1982*
UK: VERTIGO 800062-2
1 + 9 + 8 + 2 *1982*
UK: VERTIGO 800035-2
Hello *1974*
UK: VERTIGO 8481722
If You Can't Stand
The Heat *1978*
UK: VERTIGO 8480982
In The Army Now
1986
UK: VERTIGO 8300492
Never Too
Late/Back To Back
1981/1983
UK: VERTIGO 8488002
On The Level *1975*
UK: VERTIGO 8481742

Piledriver *1972*
UK: VERTIGO 8481712
Quo/Blue For You
1974
UK: VERTIGO 8480892
Rock 'Til You
Drop*1992*
UK: VERTIGO 510341-2
Rockin' All Over
The World *1977*
UK: VERTIGO 8481732
Rockin' All Over
The Years *1990*
UK: VERTIGO 8467972
Whatever You
Want/Just
Supposin'
1979/1980
UK: VERTIGO 8480872

STOOGES
Funhouse *1970*
UK/US: UNAVAILABLE

STRYPER
Against The Law
1990
US: HOLLYWOOD 61187-2
Can't Stop The Rock
1990
UK: HOLLYWOOD HWDCD8
US: HOLLYWOOD 61106-2
In God We Trust
1988
UK: MUSIC FOR NATIONS
CDENV-501
US: HOLLYWOOD 61186-2
To Hell With The
Devil *1986*
UK: MUSIC FOR NATIONS
CDMFN-70
US: HOLLYWOOD 61185-2

Soldiers Under
Command *1983*
UK: MUSIC FOR NATIONS
CDMFN-72
US: HOLLYWOOD 61184-2
The Yellow And
Black Attack *1984*
US: HOLLYWOOD 61183-2

TESLA
Five Man Acoustical
Jam *1990*
UK: GEFFEN: 924311-2
US: GEFFEN GEFD-24311
The Great Radio
Controversy *1989*
UK: GEFFEN: 924224-2
US: GEFFEN GEFD-24224
Mechanical
Resonance *1987*
UK: GEFFEN 924120-2
US: GEFFEN GEFD-24120
Psychotic Supper
1991
UK: GEFFEN: 24424
US: GEFFEN GEFD-24424

THIN LIZZY
Bad Reputation *1977*
UK: VERTIGO 842434-2
US: ISLAND 842434-2
Black Rose *1979*
UK: VERTIGO 830392-2
Chinatown *1980*
UK: VERTIGO 830393-2
Dedication *1991*
UK: VERTIGO 8488192
US: MERCURY 848530-2
Fighting *1975*
UK: VERTIGO 842433-2
US: ISLAND 842433-2
Jailbreak *1976*

UK: VERTIGO 822785-2
US: POLYGRAM 822785-2
Johnny The Fox
1976
UK: VERTIGO 822687-2
US: POLYGRAM 822687-2
Live And Dangerous
1978
UK: VERTIGO 8380302-
US: WARNER BROS 3213-2
Night Life *1974*
UK: VERTIGO 838029-2**Thin**
Lizzy *1971*
UK: DECCA 8205282
US: POLYGRAM 820528-2
Thunder And
Lightning *1983*
UK: VERTIGO 8104902
Vagabonds Of The
Western World *1973*
UK: DERAM 820969-2
US: POLYGRAM 820969-2

THOR
Keep The Dogs
Away *1978*
UK/US: UNAVAILABLE

THUNDER
Back Street
Symphony *1990*
UK: EMI CDP 7936142
US: GEFFEN GEFD-24354
Laughing On
Judgement Day *1992*
UK: EMI CDP 7999092

TWISTED SISTER
Come Out And Play
1985
UK: ATLANTIC 781275-2
Love Is For

Suckers 1987
UK: ATLANTIC 781772-2

UFO
Force It 1975
US: CHRYSALIS F21Y-21074
High Stakes And Dangerous Men
1991
UK: ESSENTIAL ESSCD-178
Lights Out 1977
UK: EPISODE LUSCD-9
US: CHRYSALIS F21Y-21127
No Heavy Petting
1976
UK: UNAVAILABLE
US: CHRYSALIS F21Y-21103
Obsession 1977
US: CHRYSALIS F21Y-21102
Strangers In The Night 1979
UK: CHRYSALIS CCD-1209
US: CHRYSALIS F22S-21209

STEVE VAI
Flex-able 1984
UK: FOOD FOR THOUGHT GRUB 3
US: AKASHIC 777
Passion And Warfare
1990
UK: FOOD FOR THOUGHT GRUB 17
US: RELATIVITY 1037-2

VAN HALEN
1984 1984
UK: WARNER BROS 923985-2
US: WARNER BROS 239485-2
5150 1986
UK: WARNER BROS

7599-25394-2
Diver Down 1982
UK: WARNER BROS 3677-2
Fair Warning 1981
UK: WARNER BROS 923540-2
For Unlawful Carnal Knowledge 1991
UK: WARNER BROS 7599-26594-2
US: WARNER BROS 26594-2
Live: Right Here, Right Now 1993
UK: WARNER BROS 265-2
OU812 1988
UK: WARNER BROS 7599-25732-2
Van Halen 1978
UK: WARNER BROS 256 470
US: WARNER BROS 3075-2
Van Halen II 1979
UK: WARNER BROS 3312-2
Women And Children First 1980
UK: WARNER BROS 923 415-2
US: WARNER BROS 3415-2

VENOM
At War With Satan
1984
UK: CASTLE COMMUNICATIONS CLACD256
US: RELATIVITY 8031 2
Black Metal 1982
UK: CASTLE COMMUNICATIONS CLACD254
US: RELATIVITY 8030 2
Temples Of Ice 1991
UK: UNDER ONE FLAG CDFLAG 56
Welcome To Hell
1981
UK: CASTLE COMMUNICATIONS

CLACD255
US: RELATIVITY 8032-2

WARRANT
Cherry Pie 1990
UK: CBS 4671902
US: COLUMBIA CK-45487
Dog Eat Dog 1992
UK: CBS 4720332
US: SONY MUSIC 52584

WARRIOR SOUL
Drugs, God And The New Republic
1991
UK: GEFFEN GED 24389
US: GEFFEN GEFD-24389
Last Decade Dead Century 1990
UK: GEFFEN 7599-24285-2
US: GEFFEN GEFD-24203
Salutations From The Ghetto Nation
1992
UK: GEFFEN GED 24488

W.A.S.P.
The Crimson Idol
1992
UK: CAPITOL CDP 7994432
The Headless Children 1989
UK: CAPITOL CDFA 3261
Inside The Electric Circus 1987
UK: CAPITOL CDFA 3238
The Last Command
1985
UK: CAPITOL CDFA 3218
Live... In The Raw
1986
UK: CAPITOL CDFA 3249

W.A.S.P. 1984
UK: CAPITOL CDFA 3201

WHITESNAKE
1987 1987
UK: EMI CDP 7467022
Come An' Get It
1981
UK: EMI CDFA 3219
US: GEFFEN GEFD 24167
Live... In The Heart Of The City 1980
UK: EMI CDFA 3272
US: GEFFEN GEFD 24168
Lovehunter 1979
UK: EMI CDFA 3095
Ready An' Willing
1980
UK: EMI CDFA 3134
Saints 'N' Sinners
1982
UK: EMI CDFA 3177
US: GEFFEN GEFD 24173
Slide It In 1983
UK: EMI CDP 7900082
US: GEFFEN GEFD 4018
Slip Of The Tongue
1990
UK: EMI CDP 7935372
US: GEFFEN GEFD 24249
Trouble 1978
UK: FAME CDFA 3234

WOLFSBANE
All Hell's Breaking Loose Down At Little Kathy Wilson's Place 1990
UK: DEF AMERICAN 846 967-2
Down Fall The Good Guys 1991
UK: DEF AMERICAN 510 413-2

Live Fast, Die Fast
1989
UK: DEF AMERICAN 838 486-2

ZZ TOP
Afterburner 1985
UK: WARNER BROS K9253422
The Best Of ZZ Top 1980
UK: WARNER BROS K256598
US: WARNER BROS 3273 2
Deguello 1979
UK: WARNER BROS K256701
Eliminator 1983
UK: WARNER BROS W37742
Fandango 1975
UK: WARNER BROS K256604
Greatest Hits 1992
UK: WARNER BROS 7599268462
US: WARNER BROS 26846-2
Recycler 1990
UK: WARNER BROS 7599262652
US: WARNER BROS 26265-2

index

Page numbers in italics refer to captions to illustrations

acknowledgements

Photographs reproduced by kind permission of London Features International/G. Dubose, Kevin Cummins, Jan Goedefroit, Curt Gunther, Gie Knaeps, Kevin Mazur, Ilpo Musto, Ken Regan and Derek Ridgers; special photography by Rupert Horrox.

Front jacket: Pictorial Press.
Back jacket: Rex Features, Retna/Jay Blakesberg, Pictorial Press/Keuntje, Rex Features, Retna/M. Putland.